Skunk Cabbage, Sundew Plants, and Strangler Figs

And 18 More of the Strangest Plants on Earth

Sally Kneidel

John Wiley & Sons, Inc.

New York • Chichester • Weinheim • Brisbane • Singapore • Toronto

Published by John Wiley & Sons, Inc.
Published simultaneously in Canada

Design and production by Navta Associates, Inc.

The publisher and the author have made every reasonable effort to ensure that the experiments and activities in this book are safe when conducted as instructed but assume no responsibility for any damage caused or sustained while performing the experiments or activities in the book. Parents, guardians, and/or teachers should supervise young readers who undertake the experiments and activities in this book.

Library of Congress Cataloging-in-Publication Data:

Kneidel, Sally Stenhouse.
    Skunk cabbage, sundew plants and strangler figs : and 18 more of the strangest plants on Earth / Sally Kneidel.
       p.   cm.
       ISBN 0-471-35713-8 (pbk. : alk. paper)
       1. Plants—Juvenile literature. [1. Plants.] I. Title: Skunk cabbage, sundew plants, and strangler figs. II. Title.

    QK49 .K59   2001
    580—dc21   00-051311

Printed in the United States of America

10 9 8 7 6 5 4 3 2 1

Contents

—1—

Introduction

—7—

Part One

Strange Plants That You Can Probably Find

Skunk Cabbages 9

Mosses 13

Ferns 18

Duckweeds 24

Epiphytes 29

Dandelions 34

Mistletoe 39

—43—

Part Two

Strange Plants That You Might Find

Venus's-Flytraps 45

Sundew Plants 48

Pitcher Plants 53

Giant Sequoias 59

Mangroves 65

Orchids 71

Saguaro Cactus 77

—83—
Part Three
Strange Plants That You Probably Won't Find

Giant Amazon Water Lilies 85

Bladderworts 89

Acacia Trees 92

Giant Kelp Forests 96

Rafflesias 101

Underground Orchids 105

Strangler Figs 109

—113—
Resources

—115—
Glossary

—120—
Index

Introduction

Plants Are Wild

When I was a kid, I felt that there were basically two kinds of **plants**—grass and trees. Just as there were basically two kinds of ice cream, chocolate and vanilla. True, I was aware of lime sherbet because my dad bought me some every Sunday. And I was aware of nandina bushes after my friend Nancy got a bunch of nandina berries stuck up her nose and had to go to the doctor. But those were minor variants from the basic plan.

I know now that there are an almost infinite variety of ice cream flavors, from bubble gum to jamoaca almond fudge. And there are an almost infinite variety of plants. Some are tiny specks, others are taller and heavier by far than any other living things. And most of them are not grasses or trees. Plants live wild and crazy lives, daring lives. Some of them kill and eat animals. There are plants that live as parasites. Some plants steal. Some form partnerships with animals. Plants can fly or glide, hitch rides, float, hibernate, grow fur, get naked, and play all sorts of tricks to get what they need. They can look like things they're not, smell like things they're not, and promise things they don't have, in order to lure prey or pollinators.

Lots of plants never touch the ground. Others touch the ground only after they're already hundreds of feet long. Some have whole **communities** of animals living inside them. Plants can and will amaze you. In the plant kingdom you will find the same dramas as in the animal kingdom, just acted out a little more slowly. You will meet many of these astonishing plants in the chapters of this book.

We Like Plants

Plants are interesting, and they're also pleasant to be around. We enjoy their bright and cheerful colors, their scents (some of them), and their shade. Plants are comforting, because we're accustomed to being surrounded by them. Cities with trees and flowers seem prettier and friendlier. Homes with big houseplants seem warmer and more attractive. Imagine Earth without any plants. It would be a bare, rocky place like the surface of the Moon. Such a place seems hostile and uncomfortable. We love plants!

We Need Plants

Plants are not only lovable, they are also necessary for our survival. They give us life itself. We are completely dependent upon plants for food, and so is almost every other animal on Earth. You may have studied **food webs** or food chains in school. A food web is a diagram showing who eats what in nature. Plants are at the base of almost every food web. Most animals eat plants in some form. Such animals are called **herbivores.** Some animals don't eat plants, but they are still dependent upon plants. Because the animals that they eat (their **prey**) are herbivores. Or maybe they prey upon animals that eat herbivores.

The reason we are all so dependent upon plants for food is that only plants can use the energy of the Sun to change water and a gas from our air into sugars and starches. That's where all sugars and starches on the planet come from. Animals need sugars and starches to live. We are unable to make these vital foods, so we have to get them by eating them. Sugars and starches are made in the green leaves and stems of plants. This process is called **photosynthesis.** Photosynthesis produces not only sugars, but also oxygen gas. Oxygen gas is what we must breathe to stay alive. Where do you think the oxygen on our planet came from? It came from plants. So we have plants to thank for our breathing as well as our food. Not to mention our homes. Virtually all modern homes are built upon wood frames, even though the outer layer may be brick or siding. And let's not forget our fuel. Natural gas, oil, gasoline, and coal are all derived from ancient dead plants compressed far underground. And, of course, clothes. The cotton in our clothes comes from cotton plants. Wool comes from sheep, and sheep eat plants.

The First Plants

Given our dependence on plants for so many of our very basic needs, it may not surprise you to learn that plants were on Earth long before animals. They **evolved** from algae that lived in the oceans. Over millions of years, some of the algae and simple plants living on the edges of the oceans developed coverings that kept them from drying out. Slowly they spread out into the landscape of barren rock. But they were still limited to wet environments, near rivers and streams, because they needed water to reproduce. They were very much like the algae and mosses of today. They had **sperm** cells from male plant parts that had to swim through water to reach the **eggs** in the female plant parts.

Gradually, over millions of years, horsetails, club mosses, and ferns evolved from these simple plants. Many of them grew to tree size, and they were the dominant plants during the Carboniferous period and the early period of dinosaurs. (Read more about them in the fern chapter.) But they still had swimming sperm that needed at least a film of water in order to swim to the egg.

Plant Reproduction on Dry Land

In order to truly invade dry land and establish themselves all over Earth, plants needed a way of reproduction that would enable sperm cells to reach egg cells without having to swim all the way. This major step occurred with the evolution of cone-bearing plants and then flowering plants. These two major groups of plants package their sperm cells inside tiny **pollen** grains, where they are protected from dry air. In plants such as pines, spruce, and fir, pollen is produced by male **cones**. Some of this pollen is carried by wind to a female cone, where there are egg cells. When the eggs are fertilized, seeds develop. After the seeds mature, they drop out of the female cones and can grow into new plants.

Flowers

Flowering plants are by far the most advanced, most successful, and most abundant plants on Earth. In flowering plants, pollen is produced by male structures arranged around the center of a **flower.** These male structures are often tall, thin stalks with knobs on top. A single flower usually has several, maybe dozens. The knobs (called **anthers**) are covered with grains of pollen. The stalk (called a **filament**) is just to hold the anther up high. An anther and filament together are called a **stamen.**

Basic flower parts

The female part of a flowering plant is usually at the center of a flower. It is called a **pistil** and is often shaped like a vase. A flower may have only one pistil, several separate pistils, or several joined together to form a compound pistil. A flower may have only female parts, only male parts, or both.

Since the sperm of flowering plants are packaged in pollen grains, they must rely on some method other than swimming to travel to their destination, the egg. Sometimes wind carries the powdery pollen to its destination, as in the cone-bearing plants. But some flowering plants rely on insects and other animals to carry the pollen for them. Plants that rely on insects must attract the insects somehow. That's why a lot of flowers produce **nectar**, a sweet liquid that many insects love to drink. Flowers that produce nectar often have brightly colored **petals** and a scent that appeals to insects. The colorful petals and the scent are like a billboard that says to insects and hummingbirds: "NECTAR AVAILABLE HERE."

The female pistil of a flower has been designed by evolution to receive and hang on to pollen. The bottom part of the vase-shaped pistil is a roundish **ovary**, containing a tiny egg or eggs. Each egg is inside a small **ovule**. An ovary may contain many ovules and eggs. Above the ovary is a long, slim neck, called a **style**. Atop the style is a sticky surface called the **stigma**. The stigma catches pollen grains brought by the wind or by visiting animals. The pollen grain then produces a long, thin pollen tube, which grows right down through the long style into the ovary. The two sperm cells in the pollen grain swim, protected, down the pollen tube into the ovary, where one of them fertilizes an egg. The stigma, style, and ovary together are the pistil.

Seeds

The fertilized egg and the ovule develop into a seed. Seeds are produced only by cone-bearing plants and flowering plants. A seed has wonderful advantages over the spore of a moss, a fern, or other more primitive plants. A seed contains a tiny plant ready to grow when conditions are right. It contains stored starches to nourish the tiny plant until it can grow its first leaves and begin making its own food from photosynthesis. A seed also contains a seed coat to protect the tiny plant and its food while they travel in some manner to a place where the seed can **germinate**, or begin to grow. The tiny plant, or **embryo**, develops from the fertilized egg, while the starch, seed coat, and other tissues around the embryo develop from the other parts of the ovule.

Fruits

Flowering plants have advantages over other plants, including cone-bearers. The ovary where the seed was fertilized often develops into a **fruit** that surrounds the seed or seeds. If you've ever planted cucumbers or squash or melons in a garden, you may have seen that the base of the flower (which is the ovary) is the very same thing that develops into the fruit later on. It just gets bigger, as the other flower parts wither and fall away. (Cucumbers, squash, and melons are all fruits because they all contain seeds.)

Why should a plant bother to make a fruit around its seeds when each seed already has starches inside the seed coat to nourish the little embryo? The purpose of the fruit is to attract animals that will eat it and then carry the seed(s) away from the parent plant. Animals may swallow the seeds, but the seeds often pass through the animals' bodies unharmed. Sometimes they are dropped in a new place where they will not be crowded by their relatives. This spreading out to avoid crowding is called **dispersal.**

Not all seeds are contained within fruits. Many have other ways of dispersing, such as catching the wind, or hooking themselves to animals' fur.

Petals and Sepals

The female pistil and the male stamen are the most important parts of a flower because they form the seed. But the petals are important, too, because their bright colors attract **pollinators,** such as insects. All of the petals together form a sort of tube or circle around the pistil and stamens. The circle of petals is called a **corolla.**

While the flower is still just a bud, it is covered with green, leaflike things called **sepals.** As the flower blooms, the **sepals** and then the petals open up and spread out. In a mature flower, the ring of green sepals lies outside of or under the ring of petals. The sepals all together are called the **calyx.**

Leaves, Stems, and Roots

Flowers are pretty and are key to a flowering plant's reproduction, but they are not the only important plant parts. **Leaves** are important because they have tiny structures inside their cells that carry out photosynthesis. These structures are called **chloroplasts.** Leaves also let gases in and out of plants, through tiny openings called **stomata** (singular **stoma**). These openings control the loss of water vapor from a plant. Sometimes the stomata are open, sometimes they are closed, depending on whether conditions are moist or dry, light or dark.

Stems are another important plant part. They provide support, and they contain the **vascular system** of a plant. The vascular system consists of tubelike cells, connected end to end, that move water, minerals, and nutrients from one plant part to another. They carry water from the roots to the leaves, carry sugars from the leaves to other areas, and so on. Green stems also can be important for photosynthesis. Sometimes all of a plant's photosynthesis occurs in the stem, as in the saguaro cactus you'll read about in this book.

Plant **roots** are important because they anchor plants in the ground. They also absorb water and minerals from the soil. Roots have tiny hairlike outgrowths called **root hairs** that help with absorption.

Classification

Scientists divide living things into six kingdoms: animals, plants, protists, fungi, and two that consist only of bacteria (archaebacteria and eubacteria). All of the plants in this book are in the plant kingdom, except for giant kelp. Kelp are algae. Algae make their own food by photosynthesis and they used to be considered plants. But now they are placed in the protist kingdom with the one-celled organisms.

Each kingdom of living things is divided into several **phyla** (singular **phylum**). Phyla are divided into classes, classes into orders, and orders into **families**. This book doesn't talk much about phyla, classes, and orders, but families are mentioned frequently. You can learn to recognize some of the plant families. For example, the family Asteraceae (the asters and daisies) contains all of those plants whose flowers are very much like daisies. You'll learn more about the structure of these flowers in the dandelion chapter.

Several plants in the book are in the arum family—the titan arum, skunk cabbage, and jack-in-the-pulpit. You'll learn that flowers of these plants have some odd structures, such as spathes and spadixes, that other flowers do not have.

Families are divided into **genera** (singular **genus**) and within each genus are usually several related species. I know you've heard the word *species*. A species is a group of organisms that are capable of interbreeding, or mating, with each other.

How This Book Is Organized

Each chapter in this book covers a particular species or group of plants. The first section of each chapter tells you something strange about the plant. The second section tells you what the plant looks like. The third section tells you why the plant has its odd feature, or how it does what it does. The fourth section tells you where the plants are found. The fifth section, where applicable, tells you something you can see and do with the plant (if it is one that you might actually see).

Words that are in the glossary are in boldface type the first time they appear in the text.

The "Resources" section lists biological supply companies that sell some of the plants in this book, particularly the carnivorous ones. It also lists some popular companies that sell seeds by mail. Here you will also find a list of public botanical gardens and arboretums so that you can see for yourself some of the more unusual plants that you'll read about in this book.

Part I

Strange Plants That You Can Probably Find

Skunk Cabbages

That's Strange!

You're walking along the edge of a swamp in late winter, enjoying the bright sun and the chill air. A woodpecker raps on a dead tree, with a loud rat-a-tat-tat. A couple of squirrels tear after each other, up and down a nearby tree trunk. A few of the trees are getting buds on their branches. Although there is still snow on the ground in patches, you feel the promise of spring.

All of a sudden you smell something awful. It's a skunk! Where is it coming from? You stand perfectly still, listening for the movement of an animal. You scan the woods and swampy ground around you. Where is the culprit?

You move your feet to turn and the stench hits your nostrils again. You look down. Under your feet is a broken red plant, an odd-looking thing. A couple of small flies buzz around it. Could a plant be the source of that gagging smell?

skunk cabbage in winter woods

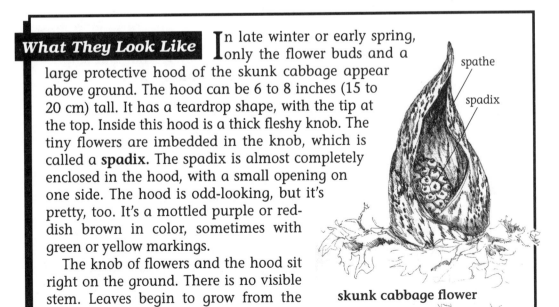

What They Look Like In late winter or early spring, only the flower buds and a large protective hood of the skunk cabbage appear above ground. The hood can be 6 to 8 inches (15 to 20 cm) tall. It has a teardrop shape, with the tip at the top. Inside this hood is a thick fleshy knob. The tiny flowers are imbedded in the knob, which is called a **spadix**. The spadix is almost completely enclosed in the hood, with a small opening on one side. The hood is odd-looking, but it's pretty, too. It's a mottled purple or reddish brown in color, sometimes with green or yellow markings.

The knob of flowers and the hood sit right on the ground. There is no visible stem. Leaves begin to grow from the

spathe

spadix

skunk cabbage flower

same spot in the soil soon after the hood and flowers are mature. At first the light green leaves are rolled into tight, pointed cones, about 4 to 6 inches (10 to 15 cm) tall. Each cone swells up like a head of cabbage, then unfolds into a coarse, floppy leaf with no stem. The leaves grow to be 1 to 2 feet (30 to 60 cm) tall. The flowers and hood die as the leaves grow. The leaves die in autumn.

Skunk cabbage belongs to the arum family, Araceae. In this family, the flowers are always clustered on a spadix. The small flowers never have petals. They do have female reproductive parts (pistils) or male reproductive parts (stamens). Each skunk cabbage flower produces female parts first, and then male parts. The tiny flowers of a skunk cabbage plant are **pollinated** by insects even though they lack colorful petals to attract them. Insects such as flies and bees are attracted by the color of the hood instead, and by odor. A skunk cabbage smells like a skunk! Many insects are attracted to foul odors. When the plant is broken or stepped on, the odor grows even stronger.

Why Do They Do That?

There are a few strange things about the skunk cabbage, not just the smell. For one thing, why does the skunk cabbage have a hood? The hood is not actually part of the flower, although it may seem to be. It just covers the flowers. What purpose does it serve? The hood is made of a spongy material with air pockets in it, so it works as an insulator. That means it keeps the rest of the plant warm. Sleeping bags, down jackets, birds' feathers, and mammals' fur all serve as good insulators because they trap pockets of air. The layer of trapped air stays warm and keeps cold air away from the warm body of a person, an animal, and, in the case of the skunk cabbage, a plant.

But skunk cabbages don't have warm bodies, do they? That's the surprising part. Unlike most plants, skunk cabbages do have warm bodies! The spadix is able to produce heat through respiration. Even in the snow of late winter, the spadix can raise its own temperature to 70° Fahrenheit (21°C) and the hood insulator helps to keep it there! The flower stays warm enough to melt some of the snow around the hood!

The skunk cabbage not only generates heat, but it seems to be able to turn the heat on and off. Researchers have shown that when the temperature drops to just above freezing (37°F [3°C]), the plants give up. They can't make enough heat to get really warm, so they just turn the heat off completely. When the air warms up a little, the plant begins to produce heat again.

Why should the skunk cabbage generate heat? One reason is to keep attracting insects. The insects can warm themselves in the warm chamber of air under the skunk cabbage hood. A very cold insect can't fly, and can't carry pollen from one plant to another. Insects that fly from skunk cabbage to skunk cabbage get warmed up at each stop, and also carry pollen stuck on their bodies from one plant to another.

Heat also causes the smelly chemicals that attract insects to **evaporate** faster. To evaporate means to move into the air as a vapor or gas. Evaporation of the stinky chemicals spreads and strengthens the odor.

When the heat melts the snow around the plant, the hood's color becomes more visible and more attractive to insects.

Heat may also make the plant grow faster. Warmth has this effect on many plants, and on **cold-blooded** animals. The faster the plant grows, the more likely it is to make seeds and reproduce successfully before it dies.

Though it's called a cabbage, like the cabbage you eat, you wouldn't want to eat a skunk cabbage (even if the smell didn't turn you off). The leaves of a skunk cabbage plant contain crystals of calcium oxalate, which cause a burning feeling in the mouth and throat that lasts for hours. The smell and the nasty chemical keep most animals from eating the skunk cabbage.

Where They Live

Skunk cabbage grows in swampy woods and meadows, particularly on the edges of swamps and slow-moving streams. When it is on the edge of a stream, where water has washed away some soil, you may be able to see the mop of roots growing out from the base of the plant. The roots look like a spray of earthworms, complete with rings around them.

Skunk cabbage is native to the northeastern United States and Canada, extending as far south as North Carolina and west to Iowa.

Jack-in-the-pulpit is found in the eastern United States and Canada.

What You Can See and Do

In autumn, you can look in swampy areas for a bud that will later form a skunk cabbage hood. The bud is 4 to 6 inches (10 to 15 cm) tall in the fall, with no spadix yet. (The hood of skunk cabbage, jack-in-the-pulpit, and other plants of the arum family is more correctly called a **spathe**.)

In late winter the hood, or spathe, gets somewhat taller and opens up a little. The spadix and flowers form inside of it. Then the spadix begins to generate heat. If there is snow on the ground, look for a purplish plant that has created a pocket for itself by melting the snow around it. If you find one, see if you can feel its warmth. Touch the outside of the hood. Then feel how thick the hood is. Don't put your finger inside the hood or touch the spadix of flowers without looking—there may be bees on it.

There is one animal that doesn't mind the smell or the foul-tasting crystals in skunk cabbage. The slimy slug. Look for round holes in the leaves that slugs have munched.

How close do you have to get to smell the skunk cabbage? What does it smell like to you?

Jack-in-the-Pulpit

You won't see skunk cabbage in anyone's garden because it stinks. But it has a nonstinky relative called jack-in-the-pulpit, also in the arum family, that is popular with gardeners. This cousin has an interesting flower arrangement, too. The tiny petal-less flowers of a jack-in-the-pulpit are on a spadix, like those of skunk cabbage. But the spadix is more slender and less knoblike. These flowers are also protected by a hood, which wraps around the spadix to form a cylinder. The spadix peeks over the top of the cylinder. In the back, the hood of a jack-in-the-pulpit extends upward and then over the spadix like an awning or a sun visor. Early settlers to this country thought the spadix looked like a preacher in his pulpit. If you lift the awning part of the hood, you can get a better look at "Jack the preacher" (the spadix).

A jack-in-the-pulpit spadix often produces only female flowers or only male flowers, but not both. And here's what's really odd—the sex of the flowers on a particular spadix depends on the condition of the plant's bulblike root, called a **corm.** If the spadix grows from a well-nourished root that has plenty of food stored in it, the spadix will grow female flowers. The female flowers have to go on to make fruits (red berries), which takes a lot of energy. They will need a well-stocked root to help them.

If the root shrivels somewhat over the year and has fewer food reserves when flowering time comes again, then the spadix may produce only male flowers. Male flowers only have to make pollen, not berries. So they don't use much energy. A given plant can go back and forth—male flowers one year, female the next—depending on the size of its root!

jack-in-the-pulpit

Mosses

That's Strange!

Imagine that you had a dog that gave birth to a litter of chipmunks. That would be pretty strange. But that couldn't happen, because all living things come from parents that are just like them. Right? Little lizards come from big lizards, little chipmunks come from big chipmunks, little oak trees come from big oak trees. That's how nature is.

Still, just for a moment, imagine that your dog did give birth to a litter of chipmunks. Imagine that, in time, the chipmunks grew up and gave birth to tiny dogs. When the dogs matured, they gave birth to a generation of chipmunks. Then once again the chipmunks grew up and gave birth to tiny dogs. Let's say that the two life-forms, chipmunk and dog, continued to take turns, or alternate. A generation of chipmunks, then a generation of dogs, then chipmunks, and so on. We could call this an **alternation of generations.**

It sounds bizarre. But some living things do have an alternation of generations. A few very simple animals do, such as some of the jellyfish. Many of the simplest plants do, including the mosses and ferns.

What They Look Like

moss growing on a tree

Mosses are usually green plants, at most a few inches high. They have simple stems, without the conducting vessels, or vascular system, of ferns, conifers, and flowering plants. The leaves of mosses are also simple and primitive. They are only one or two **cells** thick, much thinner than the leaves of the more advanced and more complex plants. Mosses have no true roots. They have tiny hairlike structures called **rhizoids** that anchor them to the ground. But like the stems, the rhizoids do not have conducting vessels. So they cannot pull water out of the soil and transport it to the stems and leaves. The leaves must absorb their own water from rain or dew on their surfaces.

Moss plants grow close together, forming dense mats and carpets. They may grow on soil, rocks, buildings, stumps, logs, or trees.

At certain times of year, a green moss plant sends up a very thin stalk, usually reaching an inch or two taller than the plant. At the top of the stalk is a tiny capsule. The stalk and capsule together are called a **sporophyte.**

Why Do They Do That?

You have probably seen green moss plants growing on rotting logs, or on the ground near your home. But these little green plants that you are familiar with are only half of the moss life cycle. They are called the **gametophyte** generation. The gametophyte is the sexual generation, which means that gametophytes reproduce sexually. At the tips of the green moss stems or shoots, small and simple male and female organs form. The male reproductive organs produce sperm cells. Each female organ produces a single egg that consists of only one cell, so the egg is very tiny. This tiny moss egg rests in a hollow area at the base of the female organ. When the mosses are wet with dew or rain, the sperm cells swim with their whiplike tails to the female organs. There, a sperm will fertilize each egg cell.

The fertilized eggs will develop into the alternate generation, called the sporophyte. The sporophyte grows directly out of the leafy female plant. It develops into a thin leafless stalk, rising an inch or two above the female plant. At the top of the structure, a capsule develops. The capsule may be almost round, or long and pointed at each end, or some other shape. Inside the capsule are **spores**. Each spore consists of only a single cell. When the spores are mature and the air is dry, the capsule will open and the dustlike spores will blow away. A spore is much simpler, and much more vulnerable than a seed, which comes from a flowering plant or a cone. But if conditions are right and the spore is lucky, it will grow into a new leafy moss plant.

This type of life cycle is called alternation of generations because the tall thin sporophyte alternates with the green leafy gametophyte. Each reproduces, but in a different way from the other. The sporophytes reproduce with spores. The gametophytes produce sperm cells and egg cells (also called **gametes**), which unite to make a fertilized egg, just as in more advanced plants, animals, and humans.

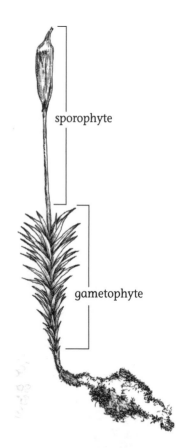

parts of a moss plant

Alteration of generations occurs in some animals, too, such as the hydrozoa. One stage is a jellyfish, which reproduces sexually. The sperm from one jellyfish fertilizes the egg of another jellyfish. The fertilized egg grows into a larva, which implants itself on an underwater surface and develops into a tiny branched structure, called a polyp stage. Young jellyfish, or medusas, develop from buds on the polyp and are released into the water to mature.

Where They Live

Mosses are found on all the continents, except Antarctica. Most mosses grow in wet or damp places. Many live in **tropical** rain forests, in Africa, Asia, South and Central America, and Australia. They often grow as **epiphytes** (see the chapter on epiphytes) on tree branches and even on tree leaves, high in the canopy where the light is brighter than on the forest floor. Mosses and liverworts growing on the leaves of tropical trees reduce the amount of light reaching the leaves. So, many tropical tree leaves shed their waxy covering every now and then to get rid of these epiphytes. The pointed tips of tropical tree leaves, called **drip tips,** help the leaves to shed rainwater quickly. As rainwater drips from the leaf tips, it carries with it the spores of mosses and other epiphytes.

In moist mountainous areas of the **tropics** (hot and humid regions near the equator), mosses and liverworts sometimes grow so thickly on tree trunks that they make the trees look much thicker than they really are.

Mosses grow in **temperate** parts of the world, too. All across the United States and Canada, mosses are common in damp shady woodlands, especially near streams. In the temperate rain forests of Washington State and southern British Columbia, mosses grow so thickly on trees that they hang from branches in great fuzzy curtains. Fallen trees in this area are blanketed by thick green and brown living mosses.

Mosses are abundant on the arctic **tundra,** too. The tundra is a vast treeless area in the far north. In winter, everything on the tundra is frozen. In summer, the top layer of soil thaws. For a short period the thawed ground is covered by very low-growing plants, such as lichens, mosses, liverworts, and short flowering plants. Mosses and lichens tend to grow in cracks and crevices that are created by the continual freezing and thawing of the ground.

There's More Than One Way to Make a Moss

Mosses don't have to make spores, or eggs and sperm, to reproduce. If a small piece of moss breaks off, it can sprout rhizoids and grow into a new plant. This is called **vegetative reproduction** or **asexual** (without sex) **reproduction.** Mosses can also reproduce by growing tiny buds, called **gemmae** (singular **gemma**). The gemmae form at the tips of the green stems or along the edges of leaves. If a gemma breaks off and falls on damp ground, it can grow into a new moss plant (a leafy gametophyte).

Sphagnum Bogs

Certain kinds of moss grow in cool, wet, treeless places called **bogs.** Bogs are found in North America, Ireland, Scotland, northern England, northern Europe, Russia, and the southern tip of Argentina. The mosses that grow in bogs are called bog mosses or sphagnum mosses. There are several different species, all in the genus *Sphagnum.* Each species prefers slightly different conditions. In a sphagnum bog, a thick mat of spongy mosses completely covers the ground. They form mounds and hollows, with shallow pools. When the mounds grow too tall, the mosses at the top dry out and die. Then the mound collapses, forming a hollow with a pool. Mosses then grow toward the center of the pool, until the pool fills in with moss. More moss grows over it, and a new mound forms. Then the mound falls in again, and so on, in a cycle. Over time, the dead moss plants in a bog build up underneath the living ones. The spongy layer of dead plant matter is called **peat.** In places like Ireland and western Scotland, where large areas of the land are treeless sphagnum bogs, people dig up the peat in blocks, dry it, and use it for fuel in fireplaces and wood stoves. It burns longer than the same amount of wood, but not as long as coal. Of the five sphagnum species involved in forming the pools and mounds of a sphagnum bog, two are green and three are reddish. Peat, composed of dead mosses, is brown.

The traditional use of peat for household cooking and heating has not been a problem, because only small amounts have been taken. But peat is now dug up by big machines for commercial use. It is bagged and sold as a soil additive for gardens. It is also sold as fuel. Huge quantities are taken and peat bogs all over the world are in danger of being permanently destroyed.

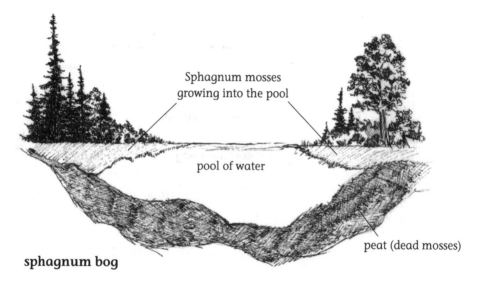

Sphagnum mosses growing into the pool

pool of water

peat (dead mosses)

sphagnum bog

What You Can See and Do

If you live in a place where there are streams and moist woodlands nearby, then you will probably be able to find mosses. Look on the ground in damp, shady areas, and on rotting logs and shaded walls. It's easy to tell if an area of moss on the ground or on a log has spore capsules. The stalks of the spore capsules will be sticking way above the green mat of the mosses, like tiny flags on long flagpoles. There will be hundreds of stalks, spaced roughly ½ inch (1 cm) apart. The stalks may be so dense that they appear at first glance as a sort of brown fuzz over the mosses.

When you see a bunch of spore capsules, pick up a clump of moss and look closely. Can you see that the stalk of the sporophyte comes from the top of the moss and not straight out of the ground? Measure the height of a few stalks and the length of a few capsules. Are all of the sporophytes the same height? Probably not, but they will be close in size. Are the capsules all the same shape? They should all be very similar.

If you notice a different kind of moss with sporophytes, measure the height of the stalks and the length of the capsules. Observe the shape of the capsules. How do the shape and measurements compare to those of your first moss? Mosses are not nearly as easy to tell apart as flowering plants, but you can become an expert at recognizing the species you've examined and measured.

Ferns

That's Strange!

Imagine you are wandering through a sparsely wooded landscape in the late Jurassic period, 150 million years ago. There are no other humans around. Humans will not appear on earth for another 148 million years at least. But there are plenty of dinosaurs. In the distance you can see the long neck of a Diplodocus, as it lumbers across an open space on its columnlike legs. Much closer, you see a stegosaur feeding on mosses and small ferns growing close to the ground. It's the size of a small pickup truck, with a row of bony plates along its back. But you're not afraid. You know that neither *Diplodocus* nor *Stegosaurus* is a meat-eater.

There are lots of trees around, but they're different from those back home in the 21st century. Many of them are cycads, which look like palm trees. But some of the trees seem to be giant *ferns!* They look so odd, like giant feather dusters!

You move cautiously toward the stegosaur for a better look, and you come across several plants that look like bamboo, but with odd, cordlike leaves sprouting from each joint. They remind you of horses' tails. Where are the oaks, the maples, the apple trees, the flowers? There are none. Flowering plants, including most of the trees and shrubs we know today, won't appear

ancient landscape of cycads and tree ferns

for several million years yet. The cycads, ferns, and horsetails are already old-timers, though. They were on the scene for 80 to 130 million years or more before the first dinosaurs!

What They Look Like There are over 6,000 species of ferns alive on Earth today. Most grow on land, rooted in soil, and are no taller than 6 feet. The stems (called **rhizomes**) are usually horizontal and underground. Roots grow out from the rhizomes, and a few large leaves grow from the rhizomes upward through the soil. Usually only the leaves are seen above ground. The leaves of most ferns are intricately subdivided, giving them a lacy or feathery appearance. Fern leaves are sometimes called **fronds.**

Although short and rooted is the typical form, there are many deviations from it. A few ferns in tropical places still grow as trees, as in the Jurassic period when dinosaurs roamed. Tree ferns today can be 60 to 80 feet tall! Many smaller ferns in the tropics grow as epiphytes. This means that they grow on other plants or on trees, instead of rooted in the ground. The roots of epiphytes take in all the water and minerals they need from rainwater and from plant debris stuck in crevices on the other plant (see the chapter on epiphytes).

A few fern species grow in ponds or lakes, either on the surface or under water. The tiny aquatic fern *Azolla* is less than ½ inch (1 cm) tall.

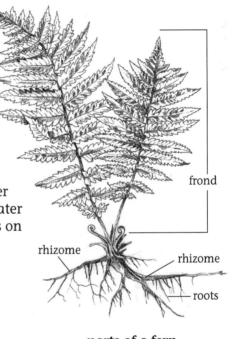

frond

rhizome

rhizome

roots

parts of a fern

Why Do They Do That?

At one time ferns and their relatives were the main plants on Earth. They were the most advanced form of plant life back in the Carboniferous period, 300 to 350 million years ago. Today flowering plants dominate on Earth. But back then there were no flowering plants, or cone-bearing plants.

Flowering plants and cone-bearing plants are so successful today because they produce seeds. A plant that makes seeds has a great advantage over other plants, because seeds are a very efficient way to reproduce. A seed is a little package that has a tiny plant inside, along with food for the little plant to help it get started. The little plant and its food are wrapped in a sturdy, almost waterproof seed coat. The seed coat keeps the little plant from drying out and protects it until the seed is able to sprout.

When conditions are right, the seed coat opens and a tiny root comes out. Then the one or two little seed leaves raise their heads. It doesn't matter if the plant can't reach sunlight right away, to make food by photosynthesis. There is enough food packed on board to fuel several days' growth.

But ferns don't produce seeds, so they don't have this great advantage. If they don't make seeds, then how do they reproduce? They make spores. A spore is very different from a seed. It's only one cell, with a thin covering, so tiny you can't even see it. When there are thousands, you can see them as dust or powder.

In a flowering plant, it is the flower that produces the seeds. In a cone-bearing plant (such as a pine, spruce, fir, etc.), the cone produces the seeds. Since ferns have neither flowers nor cones, what produces the spores?

Fern spores form in tiny sacs called **sporangia.** Each **sporangium** (singular) is so tiny that a microscope must be used to see any details of its structure. A group of sporangia looks like a brown dot on the undersurface of a leaf. These dots are called **sori,** or **fruit dots.** Many people who see them mistake them for insect damage or evidence of disease. Some fern species produce their sporangia in berrylike masses on special stalks. When the spores inside a sporangium are mature, the sporangium opens and they fall out or are blown out. Sometimes they are shot out, by a spring action in the sporangium.

The vast majority of spores land in places where they can't grow. Since they have no tiny plants already inside, and no food on board, they must have everything they need immediately at hand to get started. They need water, minerals, sunlight, air, and a moderate temperature. A spore starting to grow must have a steady supply of these things in just the right balance for an extended time.

When a fern spore does begin to grow successfully, it doesn't grow into a fern. It grows into an odd little heart-shaped plant called a **prothallus** (plural **prothalli**) or a gametophyte. The prothallus is green, paper thin, and very delicate. When it is full-grown, it is only ¼ inch (0.6 cm) wide! It soaks up water and minerals through root-like hairs on its underside. Through photosynthesis, it uses sunlight to make the food it needs.

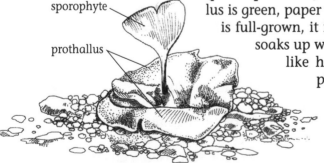

sporophyte

prothallus

a sporophyte sprouting from a prothallus (gametophyte)

So how do we get a new fern plant, if a spore produces only a prothallus, and a full-grown prothallus is ¼ inch across? The prothallus reproduces sexually and gives rise to a fern plant! A prothallus makes a single egg cell, near the middle where the two curved edges come together. Along the far edge of the prothallus, sperm cells are produced. The sperm cells swim through a film of water to the egg cell and fertilize it. Once it is fertilized, the egg cell begins to grow into a leafy fern plant. This relatively large, leafy stage is called a sporophyte because it produces spores. The tiny prothallus is called a gametophyte because it produces eggs and sperm, which are both sometimes called gametes.

A prothallus is not a very practical way to reproduce. The flat little thing is easily killed by drying out. So ferns often reproduce vegetatively, skipping the sexual prothallus stage. If you have houseplants in your home, you may have seen them reproduce vegetatively. This means that a part of a mature plant, such as a stem, leaf, or root, can give rise to another independent, mature plant. The rhizome, or underground stem, of a fern can grow for a long way underground and can produce many plants. A broken-off piece of rhizome planted in a pot of soil will produce a new fern plant. A few fern species produce small, brown, ball-shaped structures on the leaves, called **bulbils.** When a bulbil falls off, it grows into a new fern plant. In some cases bulbils even sprout new leaves *before* they fall off.

Some ferns make new ferns when a mature leaf arches over and touches the ground. The tip takes root and a new rhizome develops underground. The new rhizome sends up leaves and a new plant is created. These plants are sometimes called walking ferns.

◄ Got Vessels? ►

Ferns were one of the earliest plants to develop leaves, stems, and conducting vessels. These vessels move water, dissolved minerals, and sugars from one part of the plant to another. The vessels work in some ways like our blood vessels. This may not seem like a big deal, but it is. If modern plants did not have these vessels, then the *only* land plants we would see alive today would be small plants along the edges of swamps and ponds. No trees, no shrubs, no flowers.

The very first plants on earth were **aquatic** plants. The cells of a small aquatic plant can easily absorb the water they need from the water around them. But what about a tall plant that is not in water? The cells at the top of such a plant will quickly dry out in the air and die if they don't have a way to get water. Vessels are the answer. If a plant has conducting vessels, called a vascular system, then the roots can pull water from the soil, and the water can be transported through the vessels to the cells of the stems and leaves. Ferns were among the first plants to develop a complex vascular system. This allowed them to spread away from water and onto dry land.

Where They Live

Fern plants are found on all the continents except Antarctica. Three-fourths of all fern species live in the tropics. They range from lowland swamps to high mountains. Some live in water, others in treetops where they never touch the ground. If you are looking for ferns in the United States or Canada, look along stream banks and in other places where there is plenty of moisture. Some live in full sun, others in deep shade.

Tree ferns are found in warm areas of Central America, Malaysia, and New Zealand. They have been introduced into some southern areas of the United States.

Other Ancient Vascular Plants

There are only four groups of plants alive on Earth today that do not produce seeds, but do have a well-developed vascular system. The ferns are the biggest and best-known of the four groups. The other three are whisk ferns, club mosses, and horsetails.

The whisk ferns are the descendants of the very earliest vascular plants. They are now the simplest of the vascular plants, having no leaves or roots at all. They consist only of green, forked stems. Whisk ferns live in the tropics or subtropics.

Club mosses are small plants that look a lot like true mosses but are not related. They are often used in Christmas wreaths or other decorations. The leaves are short, narrow, and arranged in tight **whorls** around the stems. Club mosses are most abundant in the tropics or in temperate areas with a lot of rain. Over 270 million years ago, many were treelike.

Horsetails look somewhat like bamboo. They have green, vertical, jointed stems. Each stem grows out of the ground singly, and is never forked or branched. At each joint is a whorl of long, needlelike leaves that point upward. The stems arise from underground rhizomes with roots. Most are less than 3 feet (1 m) tall, but they can grow as tall as 9 feet (3 m). Horsetails appeared around 300 million years ago. Back then, many were much taller and tree-like. Horsetails are fairly common in the United States and Canada.

club mosses

whisk ferns

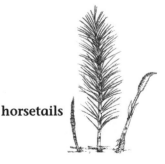

horsetails

What You Can See and Do

If you know someone who has a fern, maybe they will give you an inch or two of rhizome that you can plant. Put it in moist soil in a pot with drainage holes in the bottom. Cover the rhizome with just enough damp soil to keep it from drying out. Check the soil frequently and water it when it starts to get dry.

You can grow some prothalli, too, if you are careful to keep conditions right. If you find some ferns that have sori on the leaves, place a big piece of light-colored paper under the fern and shake the leaves vigorously. If the sporangia are mature, some will fall off onto the paper. Make a funnel with your paper and slide the sporangia into a cup or a jar. When you get home, put some sterilized potting soil into a pie pan or a clear plastic container (such as one from a grocery store deli, used to hold a sandwich or a salad). Add water to the container so that the soil is moist but not soaked. Then sprinkle your sporangia and spores over the soil. Cover the top with clear plastic wrap or a clear lid to keep the moisture in. Keep the covering loose so a little air can circulate. The container must stay in a warm, well-lit area, but not direct sunlight, which could overheat the new growth. If the soil begins to dry out, moisten it with a spray bottle of water. Or you can poke a few holes in the bottom of the container and set it in a tray of shallow water. Don't pour water on the soil, or you may wash the spores under the soil.

After about a month, you should see some prothalli growing on the surface of the soil. Be sure to keep the surface moist. Keep watching for several weeks to see if any tiny fern plants begin to grow from the prothalli. If you want to transfer one to a pot of soil after a few weeks, scoop up the little plant and the soil around it with a spoon. Make a hollow place in your potted soil to receive the spoonful of soil and plant. Keep the soil moist and keep the plant out of direct sunlight until it is several inches tall and well established.

If you can't find any ferns with mature sporangia, you can probably still grow some prothalli. Topsoil from any woodland will probably contain fern spores. Soil from under a fern plant, with or without fruit dots, will almost certainly contain fern spores from previous releases. So collect a handful of topsoil from a woodland, from under a fern if possible, and put it into a clear container. Then proceed as above. You may find that various kinds of seeds sprout in your soil sample. Remove any plants you see that aren't prothalli, being careful not to disrupt the soil too much. The prothalli may not appear for several weeks. I tried this with soil from under a fern, and I got hundreds of prothalli in one dish, but it took about a month. The very famous scientist Charles Darwin once collected a handful of mud from a pond bank and watched it for several months, keeping it moist. He recorded over 500 plants sprouting from that small bit of mud!

Duckweeds

That's Strange!

Every fall you hear about local gardeners trying to set size records with over-grown fruits. Pumpkins and watermelons can get so big that gardeners need wheelbarrows to move them. But what are the smallest fruits? Grapes are pretty small. Or maybe blueberries? Blackberries are even smaller, because each little rounded lump on a blackberry is actually an individual fruit. Surely that is the smallest fruit.

Believe it or not, the world's smallest fruit is smaller than one grain of salt! Each side of a salt grain is about 0.012 inch (0.3 mm) long. The fruit of one duckweed species, *Wolffia angusta,* is only about 0.01 inch (0.25 mm) long on its longest side, smaller than the smallest measurement on a metric ruler.

What They Look Like Not only are the fruits of the duckweed tiny, the plants are, too. The duckweeds are a family of tiny aquatic (living in water) plants. The family name is *Lemnaceae*. It consists of 6 genera and 46 species. All species of duckweeds float, either on the surface of the water or just below it. They usually occur in dense clusters, forming a thin, green mat that may cover the entire surface of a pond. A mat may contain 100,000 to 2 million plants per square yard, depending on the size of the species. Some species in the genus *Wolffia* are so tiny that individual plants are barely visible without a magnifying glass. Groups of these tiniest duckweeds look like green scum on the water.

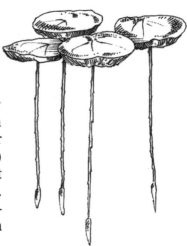

A duckweed plant of any species has a single leaf and no stem. (Scientists call the leaf a **thallus**, because it doesn't have all of the special cells that a true leaf has. But we will call it a leaf because it looks like a leaf.) The largest species of duckweed, called greater duckweed, has an oval to round leaf ¼ inch (6 mm) long. In the smallest genus, *Wolffia* (or watermeal), the leaf is only ¹⁄₂₀ inch (1.3 mm) to ¹⁄₃₂ inch (.8 mm) in diameter! That's about as big as the period at the end of this sentence. The most common species is called lesser duckweed *(Lemna minor)*. Its leaf is more oval than round, and about ⅛ inch (3 mm) long.

Some species have one or a few hairlike **rootlets** dangling from the leaf into the water.

**common duckweed
and flower**

Usually the job of plant roots or rootlets is to absorb water and nutrients. But in duckweeds, the leaf itself can absorb water and nutrients through its underside. So the rootlets' job is probably to keep the leaf from turning over.

If you collect a bowl of duckweed from a pond, you'll probably notice that each plant appears to have two, three, or more leaves. That's because the plants are reproducing, in a process called **budding.** New plants are growing off the side of a single older leaf. When five or six new plants have formed, the plants break apart. Each new one will have a single leaf and maybe a few rootlets.

Duckweed flowers are, of course, very tiny, too. They grow on the edges of the leaves. A duckweed flower has no petals, but only a single female organ (a pistil) and a few male organs (stamens) enclosed in an open sac called a spathe. (The hoods of skunk cabbages, titan arums, and jack-in-the-pulpits, discussed elsewhere in this book, are also called spathes.) When pollen from one flower fertilizes the egg inside the pistil of another flower, a tiny fruit forms.

Although duckweeds are able to make fruits and seeds, they don't often do so. Reproduction by budding is much more common. Duckweeds have yet another mode of reproduction, one that allows them to survive freezing winters. From midsummer to late autumn they produce tiny, kidney-bean–shaped buds that break off and sink to the bottom of the pond. These tiny buds are called **turions.** The turions remain **dormant** (inactive) all winter. In spring when the water warms, each turion produces a gas bubble that makes it rise to the surface, where it quickly grows into a new plant.

Why Do They Do That?

Why are duckweeds so tiny? We don't know for sure. But they may have traded size for speedy reproduction. Their small size and their very simple body form (no stem, no true roots, no complex leaves) allows them to reproduce very quickly. To make a new plant, a duckweed just grows a new thallus or simple leaf on its edge, which takes only a few days. A single plant can produce several more by budding in less than a week.

Large plants and more complex plants can't reproduce so quickly. A big oak tree might take 50 to 100 years to reproduce itself. Even familiar garden plants, such as pansies or daisies, take several weeks to produce another adult plant.

Why would duckweed need to reproduce itself so quickly? Can you guess? Perhaps because they are eaten so greedily by animals. Ducks swallow hundreds of plants in a single gulp. Maybe the duckweeds need to reproduce quickly to replace the huge numbers that are eaten every day by ducks, other birds, turtles, and the many other herbivorous (plant-eating) animals mentioned above.

Duckweeds Are for Ducks (and Beavers and Fish and...)

Duckweeds are given that name because they are eaten in abundance by ducks and other waterfowl. Surface-feeding ducks like mallards and wood ducks especially relish them. But diving ducks that usually feed underwater also eat them. Swans, coots, pheasants, and other birds do, too.

Duckweeds are very nutritious, high in protein and minerals. They are also easy to scoop up. No breaking of stems or chewing is required. Since birds have no teeth, duckweeds are an easy diet. Many fish are known to eat them, especially carp. Water turtles probably do as well. All of these animals that feed on duckweeds are actually eating much more than just the plant, because mats of duckweed harbor dozens of different kinds of tiny animals. When the duckweeds are eaten, these animals are eaten, too. One researcher found 37 species of insects in one type of duckweed. These included pond-lily aphids, springtails, tiny moth larvae, fly larvae, weevil larvae, caddis fly larvae, and the eggs of water striders and predaceous diving beetles. Many of these creatures were feeding on the duckweed, others were there for shelter.

Many noninsect creatures live in duckweeds, too, including planarians, hydra (a tiny predator related to jellyfish), and the eggs of snails and tiny **crustaceans.**

No wonder duckweeds are such a popular meal with large animals. A duckweed dinner has a little bit of everything!

duck eating a mouthful of duckweed

Duckweed–Who Needs It?

We can appreciate duckweeds because they nourish so many different kinds of wildlife. But wild creatures are not the only ones eating duckweeds. These tiny plants are also used as feed for livestock and domestic animals—especially hogs and poultry (chickens, turkeys, etc.). Even humans eat duckweed. In parts of Thailand, Burma, and Laos, the tiny duckweed *Wolffia* is grown and harvested for people to eat.

Duckweed can be helpful in other ways, too. A mat of duckweed on the surface of a pond can cut down on the growth of undesirable algae in the water. They do this by shading the water below them. Algae don't grow well in shade.

Duckweeds help with pollution as well. They are unusual in their ability to grow in water that has been polluted by agricultural wastes or animal wastes. They can even grow on "hog-waste lagoons." These are large vats or pools of hog sewage on hog farms. The hog waste in lagoons is treated and eventually dumped into nearby streams. When duckweed is grown on these lagoons, it absorbs pollution-causing nutrients from the waste. It can also be used to treat human sewage in the same way. It's inexpensive and it reduces the amount of other treatment needed. When duckweeds have finished their job in a hog lagoon, the tiny plants can be scraped up and used for livestock feed.

Where They Live

Duckweeds live all over the world, from the tropics almost to polar areas. They are found only in freshwater, in ponds and slow-moving rivers. Because they are so tiny, duckweed plants are easily carried from pond to pond by animals. The little plants cling to the fur of aquatic mammals (beavers, etc.) and to the legs and feathers of ducks and other swimming or wading birds. When these animals move to a new pond, they carry the duckweed with them. This is why duckweeds are found all over the world.

What You Can See and Do

Look on nearby ponds and slow-moving rivers in summer. If you see tiny leaves floating on the surface like microscopic lily pads, they are probably duckweeds. Gather three or four plants and some pond water in a bowl and take them indoors. Set the bowl down on a table and look at the plants carefully. Notice how the leaves float on the surface and the hairlike roots hang straight down. Push the plants underwater and see how they come right back to the surface when you let them go. Turn them upside down and they will right themselves so the roots are down and leaves are up.

Do some of the leaves appear to have more than one leaf? The extra leaves are buds. Count how many leaves are on each plant in your bowl and add up the total. Write it down. Leave the bowl in a brightly lit area, maybe on a windowsill. Or you can set it outdoors. After a few days, count the leaves again. You will probably find several more. If you look carefully, you can see that some are very small and are growing right off the edge of another leaf. Duckweeds grow very quickly. In just a few days they can double the amount of pond surface area they cover.

Look carefully at the pond water in the bowl with the duckweed plants. Do you see any tiny creatures? You may see some microscopic crustaceans, shooting around in the water, or tiny worms wiggling. You may see more after an hour or two indoors than you did at first. Creatures that were living in the duckweed may be distressed by the move indoors (change in temperature and light conditions). They may leave the duckweed and move around in the water, looking for a more agreeable spot.

Keep at least an inch or two of pond water in your bowl. If it begins to smell funky in the slightest, change it for fresh pond water. If you keep the duckweed plants all summer, they and their descendants should fill the bowl by summer's end. If they don't grow very quickly, add a tiny bit of plant fertilizer with nitrogen and phosphate in it. Add as much as the directions say for the amount of water you have. Or as an experiment, keep a few plants in a bowl of plain pond water and a few plants in a bowl of fertilized pond water. Start with the same number of leaves. After a month or so, compare the number of leaves in the two bowls. Which grew faster?

Epiphytes

That's Strange!

The small pool of water is only a few inches across and a few inches deep. But to the creatures that live in it, it is the whole universe. Every day, life's dramas unfold inside the little pool. Dead leaves that fall into the pool are eaten by bacteria and other microorganisms in the water. Mosquito larvae and other small insects eat the microorganisms. They, in turn, are eaten by larger insect larvae, such as dragonfly and midge larvae. In this pool is a single tadpole of the genus *Dendrobates*. The tadpole is lucky that there is not a damselfly larva in this pool, because if there were, the damselfly larva would probably chew up the tadpole. Still, the tadpole has to look out for birds that may visit the pool, looking for a morsel. Monkeys may stop by for a drink.

Here's a visitor now! Who is it? It's Mom! Mama frog backs her hind end up to the pool and lays some infertile eggs for her tadpole to eat. She visits every now and then to leave more eggs for Junior's lunch. She doesn't mind. It's not too far—only about 200 feet (60 meters) above the forest floor. But how can there be a pool so high up in the air? This pool is in the center of a plant called a tank bromeliad, a plant that holds up to 2 gallons (7 to 8 liters) of water! The whole plant —pool, animals, and all—is perched on the branch of a rain forest tree, in the very top of the forest.

frog in a tank bromeliad

What They Look Like

An epiphyte is any plant that grows on another plant, usually a tree. It is not a parasite, as mistletoe, *Rafflesia,* and the underground orchid *Rhizanthella* (also in this book) are. It doesn't steal food from the tree. Rather, it uses the tree only as a place to perch or a resting platform.

In tropical areas, many different kinds of plants can grow as epiphytes. You've probably seen ferns growing near your home, rooted in the ground. In the tropics, ferns often grow as epiphytes. In the United States and Canada, orchids are usually rooted, but in tropical areas, orchids are usually epiphytes, too. Because the tropics are warmer and wetter, ferns and orchids and other leafy epiphytes can survive perched high above the ground. In cooler and drier areas like most of the United States and Canada, ferns and orchids can only survive rooted in the ground. Soil provides more moisture, and it protects their roots from freezing temperatures.

Many of the tropical plants that grow as epiphytes are in the family commonly called the bromeliads. Some types of bromeliads have thick, pointed leaves with spines along the edges. These thick leaves may grow in a round **rosette** that catches rainwater in the center. Such plants are called tank bromeliads, because they hold a "tank" of water. Other bromeliads have narrow and thin leaves. Some have leaves that are very stiff and needlelike. On some, the leaves are like twisted wire.

Not all bromeliads are epiphytes. The plant that provides the familiar pineapple fruit is a bromeliad that is rooted in the ground. It also grows in the tropics. The bromeliad family is often called the pineapple family, and epiphytes in the family are sometimes called "air pines," short for "air pineapples."

Bromeliads that are epiphytes perch on the top surfaces of branches, or in the crotches of trees. Their roots may wrap around a branch. A large rain forest tree may be almost covered by epiphytes. If you see a close-up picture of a rain forest tree, look at it carefully. The epiphytes give the tree a very lush look. Leafy epiphytes like ferns, orchids, and bromeliads cannot survive in temperate areas like the United States, not even in the temperate rain forests of Washington and Oregon. It's too cold. The only epiphytes you'll see in temperate areas are mosses, lichens, and algae—plants that usually lie close to the surface of the tree, where they are not as vulnerable to drying and cold.

epiphytes

Why Do They Do That?

Why do epiphytes grow in the treetops? Surely there are more nutrients and more moisture in the soil than on a branch. For a small plant, there are several advantages to locating in the treetops. For one thing, most of the available sunlight is at the top of the forest. The treetops in a rain forest are so dense that very little sunlight gets through to the forest floor. Plants need sunlight in order to carry out photosynthesis. They use the energy of the Sun to make food from water and carbon dioxide. The product is sugar, which is then transformed into other **carbohydrates** for storage in the cells of the plant. The plant uses carbohydrates to provide energy for growth and repair.

Another reason to be up high is for **pollination.** Most bromeliads produce flowers that depend upon insects or hummingbirds to carry pollen for them. These pollinators often hang out in the treetops, because that's where most nectar-laden flowers are. There aren't many flowers near the rain forest floor, which is usually in deep shade. So epiphytes in the treetops are more likely to be visited by pollinating insects and birds.

Another advantage to being way up there in the treetops is seed dispersal. Most epiphytes depend on the wind to spread their tiny seeds around to new places. The seeds may have a little fluff of hairs at one end, like dandelion seeds. The wind catches them and carries them away. But there is very little wind on the forest floor. The wind blows up above the trees and through the treetops.

A treetop location also has its disadvantages. One of the main problems is how to get nutrients. Most plants get minerals that they need from the soil. Epiphytes can't do that. The best spot up in a tree, for a plant that's seeking nutrients, is the area where two branches come together. Plant litter gets stuck there, and bugs live in the leaf litter, making it a gold mine of nutrients. Not everyone can live in the best spot, though. Some epiphytes grow in a basket shape to catch leaf litter on their own. The tank bromeliads catch both water and plant litter. The tanks support lots of tiny animals that live in the water, including the insect larvae and the tadpoles mentioned above, plus crabs, salamanders, beetles, slugs, and worms. Lizards and small snakes can live on the plant, although not in the water. Birds and small mammals may visit the pools to drink or look for prey. Animals leave their droppings in the water. When small creatures in the water die, their bodies decay there. All this stuff makes a rich nutrient soup. The tank bromeliads absorb the soup right through their leaves, in much the same way that pitcher plants (also discussed in this book) do. The difference is that bromeliads don't trap and kill creatures. The critters just live and eventually die there.

Other epiphytes besides tank bromeliads benefit from decaying animal waste. A few epiphytes serve as ant nests. Sloppy ants are the best, because the epiphytes absorb nutrients from the food, insect parts, and dead ants left lying around. One epiphyte called the ant plant has a big, roundish body, with an interior that is full of layers and tunnels and passageways for ants. It grows on mangrove trees.

Most epiphytes don't have tanks or ways of trapping plant and animal waste matter. Instead, they are forced to get what they need from dust, dead plant matter stuck in crevices in the bark of tree branches, and from minerals dissolved in rainwater. Rain picks up minerals from other surfaces as it trickles through the branches overhead and onto the epiphytes. Some of the epiphytes grow very slowly on such a meager diet.

Another main problem for epiphytes is getting enough water. Most plants draw water from the soil, but epiphytes can't do this. One solution is to keep a body of water on hand, as the tank bromeliads do. Tank bromeliads absorb the water in their own pools through their leaves. Many epiphytes have special roots that help with water absorption. The roots are covered with dry, dead cells. When the air is dry, the dead cells act as a protective covering over the living parts of the roots. When it rains, these dead cells absorb water and swell like a sponge. The water then moves into the living parts of the roots. Bromeliads often have microscopic "parasol hairs" on the surfaces of the leaves to absorb water. The hairs look like tiny parasols all over the leaf, but they are much too small to see with the naked eye. The round part of each parasol is made of dry, dead cells and the stalk is living cells. When rainwater hits the leaves, the dry, dead cells absorb the water and pass it on to the living cells, which move the water into the leaf.

Leaves of all kinds have tiny openings called stomata. Gases for respiration and photosynthesis pass in and out through these openings. Plants can lose a lot of water through the stomata. Epiphytes save water by opening the stomata only at night, when there is more moisture in the air. Many epiphytes have hairs around the stomata that close over the holes when the air is drier, and stand back up when the air is moist.

—— Are Epiphytes Bad for the Trees? ——

Tropical epiphytes can be heavy, especially if they're holding water. The weight of several such plants can cause a branch to snap off a tree. They also cause trees to spend more of their growth energy on support. So tropical trees have many defense mechanisms to protect themselves from an overload of epiphytes. Many tropical trees have smooth bark. Epiphyte seeds have a hard time getting a foothold on smooth bark, so they seldom grow there. Most rain forest trees have oval leaves with a long, drawn-out point at the end, called a drip tip. This design causes rainwater to run very quickly off the leaf, flushing off any seeds or any bits of stuff that might help a seed get a grip. Some rain forest trees drop lower branches as the trunk grows in height. Palms are able to keep almost epiphyte-free by shedding and regrowing their branches, called fronds. Some trees even have toxic bark to discourage epiphytes. But in spite of all these measures, epiphytes flourish in the rain forest. They even grow on top of each other—fern on orchid, orchid on bromeliad, and so on.

Where They Live

Epiphytes of some kind are found in most places with trees. Places that are warm and moist have more epiphytes than places that are cold or dry. Big, leafy epiphytes such as orchids, bromeliads, and ferns grow only in the tropics or **subtropics**. Flat epiphytes such as mosses and lichens may grow on trees in cold places. In cool places with very high rainfall, such as the temperate rain forests of Washington State, mosses may grow very long and dangle from tree branches like Spanish moss does in Florida. (Spanish moss isn't really a moss, but a bromeliad!) One hiking trail in the Hoh Rainforest of Olympic National Park (in Washington) is called the Hall of Mosses, because the mosses hang so far down from the trees that they almost form walls.

Spanish Moss

Spanish moss is another tropical or subtropical epiphyte. In the United States it grows on the coastal plain all the way from Virginia down the southeast coast, across Florida and along the coast of the Gulf states. It looks like a thick and heavy grayish green beard hanging from the branch of a tree. Trees may have several clumps on every branch. It also grows on power lines, or other structures in the air.

This odd plant is a bromeliad, in the pineapple family. It's called a moss because, like a moss, it appears to have no leaves or flowers. It does have leaves and flowers, though. They are just very tiny and hard to see. The leaves are little silvery scales. Like the leaves of many other bromeliads, they are covered with parasol hairs that absorb water and transfer the water into the plant. The plant gets its minerals from this water, which has picked up the minerals from the leaves and branches of the tree. Each clump of Spanish moss is actually hundreds or thousands of individual plants!

Spanish moss was once used to stuff chairs and cushions. It is still used in greenhouses to swaddle delicate plants, to protect them from sunlight or from drying out.

Spanish moss

Dandelions

That's Strange!

The Griggs had recently moved into their first house and they were excited about having their own yard, even though it was small. Mr. Griggs planned to have a weed-free lawn, just like his neighbor across the street. After they got the furniture settled into the house, Mr. Griggs spent a Saturday afternoon pulling up every weed he could find in the front yard. He pulled up 21 thistles, 8 dandelions, and about 50 unknown weeds. Then he threw some grass seed and fertilizer over the yard. He felt good knowing he'd gotten things under control so quickly. His neighbors would soon be admiring his tidy green lawn. Now a month later, he was ambling slowly over the grass, noting with satisfaction that the grass seed was sprouting well, and there were no more thistles or unknown weeds. But he did see more dandelions. They were new dandelions, and they were in the same places the old ones were. And this time there were 27 dandelions instead of 8. How could that be? Oh well. Once again he spent a Saturday afternoon pulling them up. This time he used a hand shovel to loosen the soil, to help him get most of the roots, too. No more dandelions. For a few weeks, the lawn was weed free. Then new dandelions began to appear. This time 62 dandelions came up in the same places as the original ones! Mr. Griggs was furious. He got a big shovel and dug up every one to a depth of 6 inches. No more dandelions, this time for real. But a few weeks later he had 158 dandelion plants in his yard! He ran over to his neighbor's house, desperate. Help me!, he cried. How can I get rid of these dandelions? They're driving me crazy!

dandelion flower, seed head, and leaves

What They Look Like Just about everyone knows the familiar yellow flower of the dandelion. The leaves of a dandelion plant grow out directly from the ground, rather than from a stem. They spread out in a circle, called a rosette. Each leaf has jagged "teeth" along the edges, with a long vein in the center. In Old French, the plant was called *dent-de-lion*, which means "tooth-of-lion." That name has changed in America to dandelion. The leaves vary in length from 4 to 12 inches (10 to 30 cm).

The bright yellow-and-orange flower head is on a stalk that grows from the center of the rosette. Several flower stalks may grow from one rosette. The stalks may be only 1 or 2 inches tall, but some grow up to 18 inches or more. The flower head is 1 to 2 inches (2.5 to 5 cm) wide.

Each flower head is really 150 to 200 very tiny flowers packed closely together. Each of these tiny flowers has one yellow, upright petal, plus a female organ called a pistil, and five male organs called anthers. The pistil is a slender, vaselike structure. The base of the pistil is called the ovary. It contains a single egg. The top of the pistil, called the stigma, is forked and has a sticky surface. The job of the stigma is to collect powdery pollen. That's why it's sticky.

The five anthers are fused to form a tube around the middle and base of the pistil. The stigma sticks out of the top of the anther tube. When you look at a dandelion flower head from the side, you can see lots of stigmas sticking up above the rest of the flower head. They look like split threads or forked snakes' tongues. The anther tube produces lots of pollen. As the stigma ages, each half of its forked top curls backward, until it touches the anther tube surrounding its middle and base. If the sticky stigma hasn't already received pollen from another flower, it can now pick up pollen from its own anthers.

When all of the flowers on a flower head have bloomed, the flower head closes and stays closed for 1 to 2 weeks. Inside the ovaries, seeds develop. If you pull the flower head open toward the end of this time, you can see the seeds. A thin stalk comes from the top of each seed. At the top of each stalk is a closed parachute, made of thin, white, silky hairs.

dandelion seed head

Finally the flower opens again. Each parachute opens, too. What was once a yellow flower head is now a white ball of downy fluff, about the size of a ping-pong ball.

Why Do They Do That?

Dandelions did not grow in North America until the European settlers came. They brought the plants with them for food and medicine. Today, people still eat dandelion leaves. Young leaves that grow before the plant blooms are tender and sweet in salads. The light-colored base of the leaf is the tenderest part. Older, less-tender leaves are eaten as boiled greens, sort of like cooked spinach. The pretty yellow flowers are used to make dandelion wine. And in Europe, the roasted and ground-up roots are used to make a coffeelike drink.

But in spite of all these good points, dandelions are not always welcome. A person who is trying to grow a weed-free lawn has good reason to dislike dandelions. They are, after all, weeds. Dandelions are very successful and persistent weeds. They are *very* hard to get rid of.

What makes dandelions so successful and so hard to get rid of?

Dandelions have several qualities that make them more hardy than most plants. One thing is the rosette of leaves, spread out in a circle. The flower stems die in winter, but the rosette of leaves lives for years. Cold weather doesn't kill it. The leaves, lying flat on the ground, keep other plants from sprouting too close. So other plants don't shade it, and other plants don't compete with it for water and nutrients in the soil.

Another feature that makes dandelions persistent is the unusual root. Each dandelion plant has a very long, thick root called a taproot. It's like a carrot, except that it's crooked and branched. A dandelion taproot can grow 10 to 12 inches down into the soil. It lives for many years. If a gardener digs up a dandelion plant, the entire taproot must be dug up, too. If a piece of the taproot breaks off and is left behind, the piece will grow into a new plant. And taproots break very easily. Each piece of a broken taproot can become a new plant! You can see why a homeowner might have trouble getting dandelions out of a garden or a lawn. But the persistent rosette and long, breakable taproot are not the only reasons.

Dandelions also have an unusual ability to produce a mature seed from an unfertilized egg. Usually a flower needs pollen from another flower to fertilize the egg. When the yellow, dustlike pollen reaches the female part of the flower, the flower is said to be pollinated. Each pollen grain contains sperm cells. One sperm cell fertilizes each egg and the egg then develops into a mature seed, which can develop into a new plant.

Dandelions have all the structures they need for the complex processes of pollination and **fertilization** to occur. Yet dandelion eggs usually remain unfertilized. The eggs develop into seeds without the contribution of the sperm. Dandelions are famous among biologists for this oddity.

Where They Live

Dandelions are common in lawns, fields, pastures, and roadsides throughout much of the United States and Canada.

➤ How Seeds Are Spread About ➤

Any plant that produces lots of seeds needs to spread them around, so that they won't all grow in the same spot and crowd each other. Plants accomplish this spreading out, called dispersal, in many different ways. Seeds are often designed to be dispersed by the wind. Some examples are dandelions, thistles, and milkweeds. Others, like cockleburs or sticktights, are designed to catch a ride on animals' fur. Some, like the coconut and the mangrove, are designed to float away to new shores and islands. Some types of plants surround their seeds with sweet, moist food that animals like to eat (as in grapes, peaches, plums, apples, kiwis, figs, etc.). When animals pluck the fruit for eating, they also carry the seeds away to new places.

To see how well the tiny silken parachutes of dandelions catch the wind, pluck a few dandelion seeds on a breezy day. Hold them in your flat, open hand. How many seconds pass before all are blown away?

What You Can See and Do

Compare a dandelion flower head to a seed head. Pluck a dandelion flower head to look at carefully. Put it on a cutting board and ask a parent to slice it from top to bottom, making two halves that are mirror images of each other. This cutaway view of the flower head will allow you to see many of the tiny flowers from top to bottom. Each flower looks like a tube with a long, forked stigma sticking out the top, and a petal off to one side. Have some of the stigmas curled back yet?

You can see that the long tube is pinched in near the bottom, as though a tiny belt were tied around it too tightly. The area below the "belt" is the ovary. Pull off several flowers and look at them with a magnifying glass. Ask a parent to use a razor blade or very sharp knife to cut open one of the ovaries lengthwise. Can you see a developing egg or seed inside it yet? Sometimes you may find a tiny beetle called a weevil inside, eating the seed.

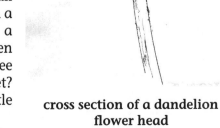

cross section of a dandelion flower head

After you've looked at a flower carefully, set it aside and then look just as carefully at a seed head. Pull out one seed and see its long, slim shape. See the long stalk attaching the seed to the silk hairs of its parachute. Now gently pluck away the seeds on one half of the seed head so that you can see the full length of the remaining ones. Do you see how they attach to the base of the flower head? Can you see that what is now a mature seed was once the ovary of a flower? What we are calling the seed is really an older ovary, with the seed inside.

dandelion seed

Examine the stems of dandelions outdoors. Measure some of the stems of the dandelion flowers and some of the stems of the seed heads that are still attached to the ground. Are they all the same? The stems often grow longer when the flower "goes to seed." This helps the seeds to catch the wind and blow away. Dandelions have hollow stems. Cut one in half. You will see sticky, milky sap flow out of the wound. Pull down strips of the cut stem as though you were peeling a banana. See how the strips curl? Most other plant stems won't do that.

Family Traits

Dandelions belong to one of the biggest families of flowering plants, the aster family (Asteraceae). You probably know many of their cousins—daisies, black-eyed Susans, sunflowers, zinnias, marigolds, chrysanthemums, thistle, lettuce, and asters. All of these plants have tiny flowers that are packed tightly into compact heads. These heads are often mistaken for single flowers. But a daisy is not a single flower. Neither is a sunflower. Each daisy or sunflower is a flower head of a hundred or more tiny flowers.

On a dandelion, all of the tiny flowers on a flower head are just alike. But many other family members have two different kinds of flowers—ray flowers and disk flowers—on a single flower head. The ray flowers grow only around the edge of the flower head. They produce a petal-like structure that sticks out from the edge of the flower. On a daisy or a sunflower, the "petals" around the edge of the flower are the ray flowers. The remaining flowers, in the middle, are disk flowers. Each disk flower produces a seed.

Why do members of this plant family cluster so many little flowers closely together? This crowding of flowers has evolved to attract pollinators. Insects and other animals that carry pollen from one flower to another are usually attracted by color and scent. A tiny flower by itself doesn't produce much color or scent. But when a couple of hundred are packed together, the effect is much more noticeable.

Mistletoe

That's Strange!

mistletoe bird
eating mistletoe
berries

The mistletoe bird on the tree branch has something hanging from its rear end. What is it? An odd little white packet, dangling by threads. The bird seems to know the hanger-on is there. It rubs its bottom against the branch and the thing comes off. Now it's stuck to the branch! But the sticky threads remain attached to the bird, stretching out as the bird hops away. Finally they break and the bird is free.

The mistletoe bird will go through this undignified procedure many times a day. Every day. The little package that was stuck to its hind end was a mistletoe seed. This is what the bird eats, its favorite diet. The sticky threads and the constant wiping are the price the bird must pay for the tasty seeds that it loves.

For the wiped-off seed, life is just beginning. The seed is now in a prime location to begin its vicious attack on the tree!

What They Look Like

There are about 1,300 species of mistletoes worldwide. Most of them grow on the branches or trunks of various types of trees. A few grow in soil, as bushes or very small trees. Some species have leaves, others don't. You may have seen leafy mistletoe used as a Christmas decoration. It is often hung at the top of a doorway. Tradition has it that anyone standing under a sprig of mistletoe should be kissed!

traditional
American
mistletoe

A mistletoe that is often used for this holiday tradition in the United States is the American species *Phoradendron flavescens*. It has small, oval, fleshy leaves and pearly white berries. Its stems and branches are green. The single European species of mistletoe, *Viscum album,* looks very much like the popular American holiday variety, and is also used in American Christmas decorations. The leaves of the European species are just a little narrower and its berries are bigger. But most people don't notice the difference.

leafless
dwarf
mistletoe

Why Do They Do That?

Why do mistletoe plants make such sticky seeds? In Australia, where the mistletoe bird lives, you'll find especially sticky and fleshy mistletoe seeds. These hefty seeds are very attractive to birds. The mistletoe bird eats almost nothing but mistletoe seeds. The stickiness is very important to the seeds' survival. That's because mistletoe plants are **parasites.** A parasitic plant is one that lives and grows on other plants, and steals at least part of its nutrition from the plant it grows on. Most mistletoe species grow on the branches and trunks of trees. In Australia, mistletoes grow on almost every native tree species. They are not like epiphytes (see the chapter on epiphytes), which simply grow on the surface of a tree without invading it. Mistletoes *do* invade their **host** trees. When a mistletoe seed is wiped or dropped onto the surface of a branch by a bird, the seed sticks to the branch as if glued there. If it weren't sticky, it would just fall to the ground and die. But it sticks and stays. Then, when conditions are right, the mistletoe seed sprouts a rootlike tip that invades the bark of the tree. It hooks up with the tissues in the tree that carry water and minerals. It cuts off the flow of water from the roots of the tree to the leaves and tips of the branches. It steals most of this water, and the minerals in the water, for itself. As you might imagine, this is not a healthy situation for the tree. If a tree has a lot of mistletoe plants growing on it, then the tree may die. A tree with parasites is weaker and is more vulnerable to insects, fungi, and diseases.

Leafy mistletoes are not complete parasites. They are sometimes called **semiparasites.** They don't get *all* their nutrition from their host trees. Mistletoes with leaves are able to trap sunlight for photosynthesis, a process whereby green plants can use carbon dioxide from the air and water from the soil to make sugar. Leafy mistletoes take only water and the minerals in the water from their host trees.

**mistletoe growing
into a tree**

Mistletoes that have no leaves are complete parasites, or **holoparasites.** Without leaves, they are not able to make sugar from sunlight. Leafless mistletoes steal sugar as well as water and minerals from their host plants. They are more harmful to their host plants than leafy mistletoes are. Leafless dwarf mistletoes infest pine trees in the American Southwest. They are common, but harder to spot than the leafy varieties. The sticky dwarf mistletoe seeds are spread around, or dispersed, when the skin of the ripe berry breaks suddenly. The seed is hurled out of the berry at a speed of 45 feet per second! It travels up to 40 or 50 feet and sticks wherever it lands. Those that happen to land on a pine tree will sprout there and will have a host to feed them for life. The others will die.

Where They Live

Mistletoe is found all over the world, except for the Arctic and the Antarctic. The more than 60 species of Australian mistletoes are very common, and found in almost every species of Australian trees. There is one European mistletoe species. In the United States, mistletoe is not very common. Dwarf mistletoe, with stems and berries but no leaves, grows in pine and juniper trees in the Southwest. Leafy mistletoes grow in a variety of trees throughout the United States and in southern Canada. Even though it is not abundant, you may be able to spot some.

➤ Almost Twins, or It's Not Polite to Mimic Your Host ➤

Many mistletoe species will **parasitize** (live as parasites on) only one or a few species of trees. In Australia, a number of mistletoe species have developed a strong resemblance to their preferred tree species. The resemblance is so strong that people often have trouble telling which leaves are those of the mistletoe and which are those of the host tree. What could be the reason behind this? No one knows for sure, but some scientists think that it has something to do with the many animals that eat mistletoe leaves. Insects such as caterpillars eat mistletoe leaves. So do many vertebrate species, such as possums. Maybe the mistletoe is hiding from these plant-eaters, by blending in with the abundant leaves of its host tree. Maybe the resemblance is a type of **camouflage**. If the plant-eaters can't find the mistletoe, then they won't eat as many of its leaves.

Other scientists have guessed that mistletoe leaves may look like the leaves of their host trees because this camouflage would force mistletoe birds to search the entire tree more carefully, in their quest for more berries. If they are forced to hop over the whole tree, they will wipe eaten berries over more of the branches in the tree. This will be helpful to the mistletoe by spreading it over more of the host tree, and making more mistletoe plants.

A third theory is that mistletoes look like their hosts because they are feeding on the host. The host tree has growth **hormones** in its tissues that control the shape of its own leaves. These hormones are probably sent to the leaves through the water that the mistletoe is taking. So the mistletoe is getting the hormones, too. Maybe the host tree's hormones are affecting the shape of the mistletoe leaves as well.

What You Can See and Do

Mistletoe is easiest to see in winter, when many of the host trees lose their leaves, but the mistletoe doesn't. In winter you may see it as a clump of small, dark leaves and branches attached to a thick limb on the host tree. It will be more or less oval in shape, and may be as big as two basketballs. It can look like a small shrub growing on one of the tree branches. If it is large and heavy, it may be hanging rather than standing upright. Mistletoe seems to be more common, or at least more visible, on tall trees with thick, heavy branches. It is often high up in the tree.

Where there is one clump, there are often more, because the seeds from one plant will infect other limbs. You may see several clumps in one tree. The seeds may also have infected nearby trees with mistletoe.

If you find a clump of mistletoe, survey the trees in the area. Has it spread to any of the others? How many? How many of the trees have more than one clump? What is the average number of clumps per tree? Which tree has the biggest clumps? Do you think it was the first one to be infected? Check the tree again in summer and see if you can still spot the mistletoe. You probably won't be able to.

If you are fortunate enough to find some mistletoe growing close to the ground, do a favor for your trees and take it off. Look carefully at the point where it was attached to the tree. Can you tell that the mistletoe and the tree were separate plants?

Do not eat any mistletoe berries. Although many birds eat them, they are poisonous to humans, cats, and many other animals.

◀━━━ The Christmas Tree ━━▶

In Australia there is a member of the mistletoe family that's called the Christmas tree. It has this name because at Christmas time, the tree is covered with beautiful golden flowers. In the area where the Christmas tree lives, December is a very hot and dry month. Most of the other trees in the area are parched and withered. How does the Christmas tree stay fresh and watered enough to produce this abundance of flowers, while everything around it is drooping?

Since the tree is in the mistletoe family, you might guess where it's getting its water. The whole tree is a parasite! The roots of the tree attack the roots of other plants underground! When an attacking root touches the root of a neighbor, it grows a little collar around the root of the other plant. The collar cuts into the neighbor's root. The fluid in the root is then channeled into the roots of the Christmas tree. So the Christmas tree prospers, while draining all the plants within 200 or 300 feet of itself.

Part II Strange Plants That You Might Find

Venus's-Flytraps

That's Strange!

Snap! The two jaws slam shut on the clumsy animal. The long, thin teeth interlock, so that escape is impossible. The jaws press closer together, crushing the creature. Digestive juices flow, slowly breaking down its soft tissues. After the resulting broth has been absorbed for nourishment, the jaws open and the remains of the prey are dropped.

Too bad for the victim. It shouldn't have been so careless around this hungry predator. And what predator is this? Alligator? Wolf? Snake? Shark? Squat little plant? It's a squat little plant—the Venus's-flytrap. Of course, they're not real jaws. They only look like jaws. And move like jaws. And capture like jaws. But the jaws are really just a leaf.

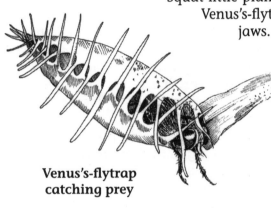

Venus's-flytrap catching prey

What They Look Like

A leaf of a Venus's-flytrap looks like a pair of wide jaws, with long, spiky teeth along the edges. The two halves of the leaf open like the two halves of a clamshell. The leaf is mostly green, but the inner surfaces can be partly or completely red. The stalk that holds up this jawlike structure is also part of the leaf, and is green. A single plant will have many leaves, all of the same shape. They all grow from a central point, like the spokes of a wheel. This arrangement of leaves, on any plant, is called a rosette.

The entire plant is usually 3 to 6 inches (7.5 to 15 cm) across and about the same in height. The leaves may lie back upon the ground, or may stand up.

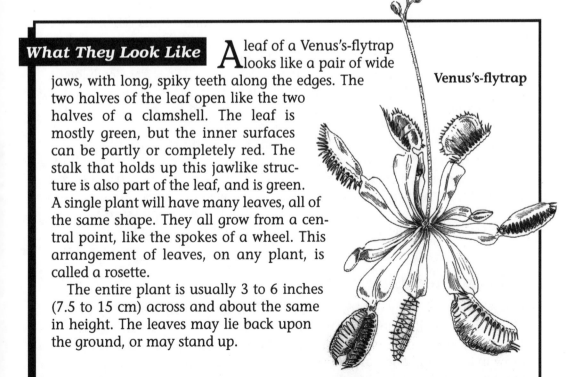

Venus's-flytrap

Why Do They Do That?

Why would nature produce such a plant, capable of capturing and digesting insects? Almost all plants are able to feed themselves by photosynthesis. They take energy from the sun, carbon dioxide from the air, and water from the soil to make sugar. Animals and humans can't do that, which is why we have to eat. Plants get some nutrients from the soil or rainwater, but other than that, all they need for nourishment is the sugar that they make themselves.

Venus's-flytraps are plants. They have all the equipment other plants have for making sugar, and for drawing nutrients from the soil. So why do they need to trap insects? Venus's-flytraps need something that they're not getting from the soil or from photosynthesis. What is it? They need more nitrogen. Venus's-flytraps grow in soil that is low in nitrogen, or they did at some point in the past. Plants must have nitrogen for growth. Most plants get this element from soil. But our squat little **carnivore** has evolved the ability to get it from insects. Insect bodies are rich in nitrogen. Trapping and digesting them helps the plant live in nitrogen-poor soil.

If the plant can't move around, how does it catch its prey? First of all, the inner surface of the leaf has many small glands that produce nectar. The nectar lures insects inside the trap. On the inner surface of the trap are a few very sensitive "trigger hairs." When two or more of the hairs are touched, or when one is touched more than once, the trap slams shut. The "teeth" along the outer edges of the leaf don't bite, but they act like the bars of a jail cell, keeping the insect trapped inside. They are called guard hairs. Then the two sides of the leaf slowly press even closer together, until the captive is tightly squeezed. The inner surface of the leaf has more glands, digestive glands, that release digestive juices onto the trapped creature. The juices slowly break the insect's body into particles that are small enough to be absorbed through openings near the glands. All except the wings and the **exoskeleton** (the outer skin), which fall out when the trap reopens.

How does the trap slam shut if the plant has no muscles? No plants have muscles, not even the Venus's-flytrap. The trap closes when the trigger hairs send an electrical message to certain cells of the leaf's midrib (the creased area between the two halves of the leaf). The message causes these cells to suddenly lose water and collapse. When this happens, pressure in other midrib cells causes the two halves of the leaf to suddenly come together, shutting the trap.

Where They Live

Venus's-flytraps occur naturally only in the southeast corner of North Carolina and a small, adjoining area of coastal South Carolina. This is a region of moist, sandy savannas. Longleaf pine trees are widely spaced. The flytraps grow in the sunny open areas between these pine trees, mixed among other low-lying plants.

You should never remove a flytrap from nature. Their numbers are decreasing and those that remain must be protected. However, you can probably buy a Venus's-flytrap from a plant store or from a biological supply company (see the "Resources" section). These flytraps have been grown in captivity from seed or from cuttings. Follow the instructions for your plant's care very carefully.

What You Can See and Do

If you are able to buy one and take it home, you can experiment with the trap. Get a broom straw, or a toothpick, or even a stiff hair, and touch one of the four to eight trigger hairs on the inner surface of the trap. These are not the same as the guard hairs that look like long teeth along the edges of the trap. Touch the trigger hair just once. One touch should have no effect. This helps the plant avoid closing every time a tiny piece of debris blows in. If you touch two hairs within a few seconds, or touch one hair twice, the trap should shut. If the touches are a minute apart or more, the trap will close very slowly. It may need more touches to finish closing. What if the touches are 2 minutes apart? Will it still close? A single trap will close for you only about 10 times in its lifetime, then it will respond no more. So you will not be able to experiment forever. If the trap closes because you touched it, and no prey was caught, it will reopen the next day.

Save one of your traps for catching prey. A fly is ideal. It must be alive though, because as it struggles it touches the trigger hairs that cause the trap to close. But flies are hard to catch alive. You may be able to catch one by putting outdoors an open jar, on its side, containing a small piece of meat. If you see a fly in it, sneak up on it and slap the lid on quickly. If you can't get a fly, try a small moth or any little bug. After the trap snaps shut, you can see the two halves slowly continue to press together until the creature inside creates a dark bulge on either side. After 3 to 5 days, the sides reopen. If prey is captured each time it closes, then a trap will close only about three times before it stops working. If the prey is very big, then it may work only once. A very big item will rot inside the trap and kill the leaf, but the rest of the plant should be okay.

Will the trap close on your little finger? It might. Try it and see.

Sundew Plants

That's Strange!

The insect flew toward the surface of the leaf, a very attractive, bright and sparkly leaf. But trouble started as soon as the insect landed. Right away something had ahold of its wing. It tried to pull away, but the wing was stuck fast. What was the problem? As the insect twisted its body, trying to free itself, the other wing and a leg stuck to something else. The bug frantically thrashed and struggled, but the more it moved, the more stuck it became. Suddenly, a bunch of tentacles were coming down on it! From every direction! Some curled around the insect while others whacked its head and body with big, sticky globs of glue. The situation was hopeless! The bug was barely able to move at all. There was nothing to do but wait for the ugly end. Wait to be slowly digested.

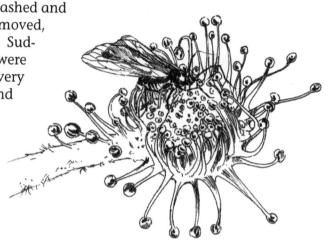

bug getting trapped in a sundew

What They Look Like The leaves of sundew plants are covered with tentacles. In the center of a leaf, the tentacles stand straight up. Toward the edges of a leaf they begin to slant outward. At the very edge of a leaf, the tentacles lie flat, sticking out around the leaf like the rays on a child's drawing of the Sun. The tentacles in the center are shortest. The longest are around the edges.

There are over 90 species of sundew plants around the world. They have a variety of leaf shapes, sizes, and arrangements. Many have round leaves; some have very long, thin leaves. Others have spoon-shaped leaves. The leaves may be in a rosette on the ground, or may be attached to tall stems. Some species have very tiny leaves, as short as $1/20$ inch (1.5 mm). But the leaves of some tropical species, such as the giant African sundew, can be 18 inches long or perhaps even longer.

The stalk of each tentacle on a sundew leaf is either red or green. At the tip of each tentacle is a small, round gland. The glands are often red. Each gland produces a drop of clear sticky liquid that surrounds it. The liquid sticks to whatever it touches. It is also stretchy, like a warm wad of bubble gum on a hot sidewalk. This makes it very hard for an insect or other small creature to break away from it.

The clear, sticky drops sparkle in sunlight, and they look like dew, like clear drops of water. Since many insects drink dewdrops, this may be one thing that attracts them to the leaves. The red color of the glands may be attractive, too. Many insects are attracted to colors. Some sundews may also have an inviting odor, as flowers do.

Sundews produce flowers at certain times of the year in nature. Captive plants may or may not flower. The color and size of the flowers vary among the different kinds of sundews. Many produce their flowers on a long stalk high above the rest of the plant. It would not be good for the plant to trap and kill the insects that visit the flowers for their nectar. They are needed to carry pollen from one flower to another, so that flowers may be pollinated and produce seeds.

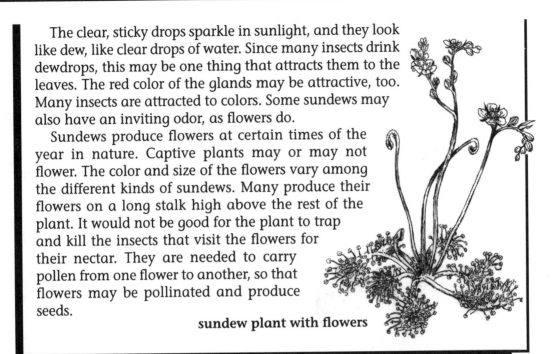

sundew plant with flowers

Why Do They Do That?

Like the Venus's-flytraps, pitcher plants, and bladderworts described in this book, sundews are **carnivorous,** or meat-eating, plants. In the 1800s, many scientists thought that sundews trapped insects in order to protect themselves from insects that eat plants. But Charles Darwin, after a series of experiments with sundews, concluded that they trap insects for their own nutrition. Sundews grow in soil that is low in nitrogen. Nitrogen is very important to plant growth.

Plants that grow in soil with little nitrogen must have some way of getting nitrogen. One solution is to steal it from the bodies of insects. When a sundew traps an insect, it absorbs all of the insect's body except for the exoskeleton, which doesn't dissolve. Much of the insect's body is made of protein, which contains nitrogen. So when the plant absorbs this protein, it gets the nitrogen it needs.

How does digestion work in a sundew? First, the glands **secrete** the sticky drops of liquid that trap an insect. A few minutes after the bug is trapped, other tentacles begin to bend toward the bug. If plants have no muscles, how can the tentacles move? A message is sent down the tentacles that are touching the insect to other nearby tentacles. The message causes the nearby tentacles to grow a little bit on the side farthest from the insect. This lopsided growth makes the tentacles bend over, toward the insect. The glands on the bending tentacles come in contact with the bug. All of the glands that are touching the insect now begin to secrete digestive **enzymes** to dissolve the bug. Your stomach also secretes digestive enzymes to break down the food you eat. As the sundew glands release enzymes onto the insect, the bug's body begins to turn into liquid. Within about 12 hours, the leaves of some types of sundews will begin to curl up around the insect. This brings more tentacles and glands into contact with the bug. It also may keep rainwater from splashing the dissolved liquid away. If an insect gets stuck on a sundew with a long, thin leaf, the leaf may wrap around and around the prey in a coil.

The gland then has a third job. It not only traps and dissolves the bug, it also absorbs it. The process of dissolving and absorbing usually takes about 5 to 14 days. When it is over, the leaf opens back up. Each tentacle then returns to its original position. After all of the tentacles have moved away, the empty exoskeleton is free to blow away in the wind.

A tentacle can move toward a trapped bug and then stand back up on three or four different occasions. After that it cannot grow anymore and will not respond to future bugs.

Where They Live

Sundews live on every continent on Earth except Antarctica. They are found in nitrogen-poor soils, often in damp or swampy soil.

What You Can See and Do

Sundews are fairly easy to keep as houseplants. You can probably find one at a plant nursery. If not, you can order one from a biological supply company (see "Resources").

One of the most interesting things you can do with a sundew or any carnivorous plant is to feed it an insect. Offer your sundew a very small insect. One that is too large can damage or kill a leaf. If a leaf on your sundew is about a half inch long, start with an insect no bigger than $1/16$ of an inch (1.5 mm). A meal that takes longer than 2 weeks to digest, or leaves brown spots on the leaf, is too big. Drop the insect onto the leaf, or put it right on the gluey end of a tentacle. A living insect will probably touch more tentacles in a short period of time, but a dead one or a piece of a dead one will work, too. Use a stopwatch to count the number of minutes that go by before you first notice movement in a nearby tentacle. Keep track of how many hours go by before the leaf starts to curl, if it does. How many hours or days pass before the curling stops? How many days go by before the leaf uncurls and the tentacles return to their original positions?

Can you fool a sundew? What happens if you put a tiny pebble or a sliver of wood or a grain of sand onto a sundew leaf? Usually the sundew will not react. Or if it does, the tentacles will return to their earlier position within a day. But what if you put a sesame-seed-sized piece of meat or boiled egg white on your sundew? The meat and egg will probably trigger the same reaction that an insect does, because they also contain nitrogen-rich proteins.

You can probably get your sundew plant to make you several more sundews that you can give to friends. Sundews are very good at vegetative reproduction. This means that a piece of a root or a leaf or a stem can grow into a separate new plant. A sundew can also reproduce from seeds, as all flowering plants can, but this takes much longer and is more difficult.

To produce more sundew plants vegetatively, remove a leaf from your sundew. Cut the leaf and the **petiole** (the leaf stem) into half-inch pieces. Put each one topside down onto moist soil in a pot, about 2 inches apart. Cover the pot with plastic wrap, using a couple of popsicle sticks to prop the plastic an inch or so above the leaf pieces. Don't put the pot in direct sunlight while the plastic is over it, or the cuttings will bake! After 2 to 8 weeks, a small new sundew plant will grow from the end of each leaf piece. Some pieces may grow two new plants.

A root will also grow new plants. In removing one, be very careful to disturb the other roots as little as possible. Cut the removed root into 1-inch

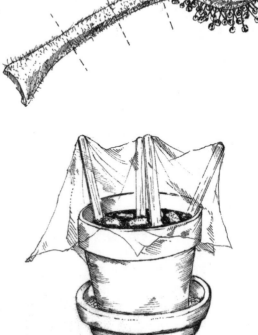

pieces and put each piece straight down (vertically) into a hole in the soil, so that one end of the root is even with the surface of the soil. A new plant will grow at the top of each root piece.

You will probably want to move a few of the best new plants into their own pots. Sundews are usually grown on peat moss or sphagnum moss. You can get these kinds of mosses at a plant nursery. They are naturally part of the growing surface in the swampy areas where sundews live. But different sundews have somewhat different requirements. If you ordered or bought a sundew, follow the growing and soil instructions that came with it. Otherwise, use a mixture of peat moss or sphagnum moss and sand. Mix together in a bucket 10 scoops of dry peat moss or sphagnum moss and 5 scoops of dry river sand (not construction sand). Some growers

planting sundew cuttings

recommend adding 1 scoop of dry African violet soil. Stir it up, then water it until the mixture is very wet. Pack it tightly into a pot or pots, a little bit at a time. Leave a half inch to an inch at the top for watering. Make a small hole in the mix in each pot for the roots of the new plant. Put the roots in the hole, then cover the roots with the moss mixture.

Sundews like high humidity. If you live in a place that is not very humid, place your pots in a tray of water about a half-inch deep. The water in the tray should be distilled water, or tap water that has been exposed to air for 48 hours so that the chlorine has evaporated. Carnivorous plants are very sensitive to minerals and chemicals in water. Distilled water has had all the minerals and chemicals removed.

Sundews like light shade or full sun, so put the tray in a sunny window. If the pot has a hole in the bottom and is sitting in a tray of water, the moss will probably stay wet. If it starts to dry out at the top, then water it at the top as you would any houseplant.

Sundews, Evolution, and Charles Darwin

Charles Darwin wrote about his experiments with sundews in his 1875 book *Insectivorous Plants*. Darwin showed that sundews will trap and digest tiny pieces of meat, but will not respond very much to nonedible objects. His son Francis continued his experiments. Francis showed that sundews that are fed meat grow bigger and healthier than unfed sundews.

Charles Darwin was a very famous scientist who experimented with many different kinds of plants and animals. He traveled around the world in the 1800s, carefully observing the variation in plants and animals on islands and in jungles and other natural areas. During his travels, he collected a lot of specimens for later study. He also studied what was known at the time about environmental changes due to movements of Earth's crust. His studies and his observations led him to an explanation of how living things change over time in response to environmental change. He called this process **natural selection.** He described natural selection and the evidence for it in his 1859 book *The Origin of Species*. The changes resulting from natural selection in a population are called **evolution.** The theory of evolution is the foundation for our understanding of biology today, so Darwin's contribution to modern science was enormous.

Pitcher Plants

That's Strange!

The wasp stops to drink a little nectar from the leaf. After a few sips, it continues strolling on the leaf. As the wasp moves around, it finds more and more nectar. What good fortune! The wasp has never seen so much nectar on a single plant—drops of nectar all over the place! But . . . suddenly the wasp is in a forest of stiff, bristly hairs! Well, no matter, they're all leaning in one direction, like the wind blew them down. The wasp can walk over them, and still reach more of the tasty nectar to take back to the workers in its nest. Yum, yum, this is nice. Hey, now what? All at once the wasp finds that it has left the stiff hairs behind. The walking surface is now smooth. And slanted. And slippery. Too slippery to walk on! Better go back. But wait—when the wasp turns around, the stiff hairs are all pointing at it like little spears. Oh no. This looks bad. Forest of spears or slippery slope? What should . . . AAAAIIIIIIEEEEE!

wasp entering a *Sarracenia* (trumpet) pitcher

The wasp has tumbled down the slick and waxy slope into an icky soup, a soup of . . . dead bugs! How will it *ever* get out?

What They Look Like Pitcher plants are insect-eating plants. A single leaf of a pitcher plant is able to trap and digest an insect. But they don't have moving parts, as sundews and Venus's-flytraps do. So how do they do it?

Each leaf forms a narrow cup that is closed at the bottom and open at the top. Most have a hood over the opening that usually keeps some rain out. The hood has another job as well. The hood and the upper part of the leaf lure insects into a trap. The bottom part of the leaf holds a pool of liquid that does the digesting.

There are many different types of pitchers in different parts of the world. All but one of the North American pitchers belong to the genus *Sarracenia*. These eight *Sarracenia* species are sometimes called the trumpet pitchers because most have tall, thin pitchers that look somewhat like trumpets.

A single plant has several leaves or pitchers. Trumpet pitchers usually grow on the ground in clumps, standing upright. Most are at least 18 inches (0.5 m) tall when mature, some as tall as 3 feet (1 m). But two of the trumpet pitchers don't stand up. These two—the purple pitcher and the parrot pitcher—grow out from a central point and then lie back on the ground.

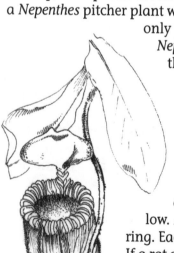

purple pitcher

The purple pitcher plant is the most common and widespread of the North American pitchers, so it is one you may see. Its leaves (pitchers) are 2 to 18 inches (5 to 45 cm) long and mostly green, with reddish areas. Most pitchers have some color in addition to green—red, yellow, or white—to make the pitcher more attractive to insects.

The flowers of pitcher plants are also colorful. The *Sarracenia* species all produce either red or yellow flowers. The single flower of each plant is perched on top of a tall stalk.

There are some very different pitcher plants found in tropical areas around the Indian Ocean, such as Madagascar, Sri Lanka, and Malaysia. These pitchers don't grow in clumps on the ground as North American pitchers do. Instead, they grow singly from long vines that climb on trees, or from long stems that creep on the ground. These pitcher plants are in the genus *Nepenthes*. Only some of the leaves on a *Nepenthes* pitcher plant will form pitchers. And when a pitcher does form, only part of the leaf is involved. Some species of *Nepenthes* have pitchers much wider and rounder than the slim North American pitchers. One species in Borneo is 7 inches (18 cm) wide and 14 inches (36 cm) long! A football could fit inside it! These are so large that they can capture and digest rats, lizards, and maybe birds, squirrels, and small monkeys as well as insects.

The leaves of *Nepenthes* are green or yellow-green, but the pitchers have flashy patterns and colors—shades of red, purple, green, or yellow. Around the top of each pitcher is a thick, ridged ring. Each ridge ends in a sharp point inside the pitcher. If a rat or a squirrel sticks its head in a pitcher to pull out an insect to eat, it might find its head trapped by this ring of sharp points. After moving around to try to free its head, the animal could find its whole body trapped inside the pitcher.

Nepenthes

How Do They Do That?

A pitcher plant doesn't have snapping jaws or moving tentacles, so how can it trap and kill an animal? Several parts of the pitcher plant work together to get the job done. First of all, the plant must attract animals. A pitcher does this with color, nectar, and sweet odors—just as a flower does. Flowers attract insects or hummingbirds in order to get pollen moved from one flower to another, but pitchers use these same tools for a more sinister goal.

An insect might come to a pitcher because it sees a bright color or pattern on the pitcher, or because it can sense the nectar. At first, it sips just the nectar on the outside of the pitcher or around the rim of the pitcher. The undersurface of the hood, which has a lot of nectar glands, is the most attractive area of the pitcher. But once the insect has moved under the hood, it is in trouble. It may already be trapped. The undersurface of the hood is covered with stiff hairs that point down into the pitcher. The hood and the hairs seem perfectly safe as long as the insect is moving toward the inside of the pitcher. But if it turns around to leave, the stiff hairs are pointing right in its face. So it moves further down the hood toward the pitcher.

Once the insect moves below the hood, it enters a smooth zone at the very top inner part of the pitcher. This area also has many glands producing nectar. But it has no hairs. No foothold at all. Splash! The insect falls the length of the pitcher into a liquid at the bottom. On the bottom walls of the pitcher are more stiff, downward-pointing hairs that prevent the insect from climbing out of the liquid. And the liquid it falls in is not just water. It's full of digestive enzymes that break down the insect's body, all except the outer skeleton. The enzymes come from glands on the inner walls of the pitcher.

Some pitcher plants, such as the lying-down purple pitcher, produce very few enzymes. But the bugs get digested anyway. The bacteria in the liquid are able to break down the insects' bodies without any help. As the insect bodies get broken down, the inside walls of the pitcher absorb needed nutrients from the soup. Like Venus's-flytraps and sundews, pitcher plants grow in areas where the soil is low in nutrients. The insect stew provides nitrogen and other nutrients for them.

Where They Live

There are nine pitcher species in North America. One called the cobra plant lives only in northern California and Oregon. The other eight are all in the genus *Sarracenia*. Seven of those eight are found only in the southeastern United States, mostly on the coastal plain of the Atlantic Ocean or the Gulf of Mexico. They all live in some kind of wetland—a swamp, bog, or marsh. The eighth *Sarracenia*, the purple pitcher, occurs on the same coastal plains but also extends up into the northeastern states, the upper midwestern states, and on up into Canada.

The many species in the genus *Nepenthes* are found in the tropical areas of south Asia and in places around the Indian Ocean—Indonesia, Madagascar, Sri Lanka, Malaysia, and others.

Four species of sun pitchers in the genus *Heliamphora* are found in the mountains of South America.

Pitchers of the genus *Cephalotus* grow in swamps and bogs of southwest Australia.

Cobra or Plant?

California has a pitcher plant called the cobra plant or cobra lily. The hood of a cobra plant curves down to cover the opening of the pitcher almost completely. The tall, thin pitcher with the curving hood on top looks very much like a cobra that has raised its upper body to strike. A cobra's neck has the same graceful curve as the hood of a cobra plant. And there is even more to the resemblance. The cobra plant has two dangling strips of leaf tissue in front that look somewhat like the forked tongue of a snake. Or perhaps a snake's fangs.

If cobras and cobra plants lived in the same place, we might wonder if the plant developed a resemblance to the snake because animals won't trample or bother a cobra. But cobras live in Asia, and cobra plants in California. So animals that might damage cobra plants are not aware of cobras. The resemblance can't help the plant. It's just a coincidence.

cobra plant

Stealing from the Pitcher

Some animals are able to visit or even live in pitchers without being eaten. Spiders may build webs inside the pitcher, to snag falling insects for their own meal. Small frogs and toads also eat insects. They may hang around the top of a pitcher plant waiting for an insect to arrive for dinner. Sometimes they slip and become a meal for the plant instead.

There are several moth species that eat various parts of the plant during the larval or caterpillar stage of life. Some eat the flowers. Some eat the roots or rhizomes. Others eat parts of the pitcher itself.

A few creatures can even live in the digestive liquid at the bottom of a pitcher. Some flies lay eggs on the upper and inner side of a pitcher. When the eggs hatch, the larvae fall into the liquid below. But they have a protective substance on their bodies that keeps the enzymes from hurting them.

Mosquito larvae are able to live in the pool at the bottom of a purple pitcher. This is a pitcher species that doesn't produce a lot of enzymes.

What You Can See and Do

Like Venus's-flytraps and sundews, pitcher plants can be purchased and kept as houseplants. Call local plant nurseries to ask who might carry them in your area. If you can't find any, you can order them from a biological supply company (see "Resources"). Pitcher plants should never be collected from nature. When one is taken from the wild, all of its future seeds and offspring are removed from that area, too. Carnivorous plants are very popular and could disappear from natural habitats. If you buy one, ask if it was raised in a plant nursery. Don't buy one that came from nature.

A plant that you get from a good nursery will probably come in the right kind of soil. Ask the nursery for care instructions, which may vary somewhat with species. In general, pitcher plants grow well in sphagnum moss, living or dead, or in granulated peat moss. Sphagnum is more often recommended. Sand from a plant nursery can be mixed with the moss, but doesn't have to be. Don't use construction sand. Place the pot in a tray of water. This will keep the moss or moss mixture wet, and will keep moisture in the air around the pitcher plant. Don't use any kind of fertilizer, because it will probably kill the plant.

You can start a new pitcher plant by separating a pitcher from the others in its clump. Remove a small piece of the root, too. Place the root in damp moss in a pot of its own.

You can also grow a new pitcher plant from just a piece of root. Cut a 1-inch (2.5-cm) length from the main root of a pitcher plant. The thick main root is called a rhizome. Be sure not to damage any of the small roots coming off of the rhizome, and leave enough rhizome intact to feed and support the big plant. Put the 1-inch piece of root in a pot of its own, in a horizontal position. Cover it with about ½ inch (1.2 mm) of damp sphagnum moss. It will grow a new plant.

If you have trouble with mold on the cuttings, you may need to treat them with a fungicide. Ask your parents to inquire at a plant nursery about that.

You may want to feed an insect to a pitcher plant. Any fly that gets in the room with the plant will probably go to the pitcher plant on its own. How long does it take the fly to find it? You can try placing an ant on the plant yourself. Some ants aren't interested in sweet liquids, so you may have to try a few times. Does the fly or ant go to areas that have the most nectar—the rim and the underside of the hood? Can you see the hairs on the underside of the hood guiding it into the pitcher? Does the insect ever try to leave?

The hood will probably keep you from seeing down into the pitcher. Some pitchers have close-fitting hoods that may even block your view of the rim. If the hood curves over so much that it creates a dark space inside, then the hood may have windows. These are clear areas in the hood that let light in. The light through these windows gives the impression that there are exit holes. But there are none.

You Can Help Save Wetlands

If you like carnivorous plants, do what you can to save our wetlands —the swampy or boggy areas that pitcher plants live in. Many people don't realize the wonderful variety of plants and animals that live in our wetlands and nowhere else. All across the United States, and the world, wetlands are quickly disappearing. With more and more people on our planet, we need more and more space for homes. So wetlands are filled in or paved over as we build highways and malls and homes. This will keep happening unless we let our representatives in Congress know how we feel about it. Write your local and national representatives and tell them. Your local librarian can show you how to find their names and addresses.

Giant Sequoias

That's Strange!

What living thing weighs as much as 100 elephants? A giant sequoia tree.

What tree was already at least 1,000 years old when Christ was born, and is still alive today? A giant sequoia tree.

What plant is as tall as a 27-story building? A giant sequoia tree.

What tree is so big that a man made a room that was 56 feet (17 meters) long inside of one, and lived there? A fallen giant sequoia tree.

What plant is so wide that a car can drive through it? A giant sequoia tree. One sequoia had a car tunnel carved through it, but has since fallen.

What is the largest living thing to ever exist on this planet? A giant sequoia tree.

giant sequoia

What They Look Like

A mature giant sequoia tree is generally 200 to 300 feet (60 to 90 m) tall, with a diameter of 20 to 32 feet (6 to 10 m). The cinnamon colored bark may be 2 feet (60 cm) thick at the base, and has deep furrows in it. The massive trunk tapers somewhat as you look from bottom to top. On a mature tree, the branches occupy only about the top third of the tree. The largest branches may be over 6 feet (2 m) in diameter and 150 feet (46 m) long. An oak tree that's 100 feet (30 m) tall and 3 to 4 feet (91 to 122 cm) in diameter is considered huge, but is much smaller than some sequoia branches!

While a sequoia's trunk and branches are gigantic, its leaves are tiny and scale-like, about 1/5 inch (0.5 cm) long. They lie flat along the stem, overlapping each other.

Like many **evergreen** trees, sequoias produce cones instead of flowers. The cones are 1.5 to 2.5 inches (3.8 to 6.4 cm) long. All cones from trees have scales, and a seed forms on top of each scale. A sequoia cone has 25 to 40 scales.

giant sequoia cones

Fire, Chickarees, and Beetles

On most cone-bearing trees, the cones turn brown and their scales open out like little flaps or platforms when the seeds are mature. You can clearly see these platforms all over a brown pine cone. When a cone is open like this, the seeds can come out. Usually each seed has a flat wing on it to catch the wind, so it can travel far from the parent tree to grow.

Sequoia cones are different, though. The cones don't turn brown or open on their own. They don't even fall off the tree on their own, but will keep growing slowly for years. The trees depend on fire or animals to open the cones. Fire dries the cones out, which causes the scales to open and exposes the seeds to the wind. After a forest fire is a good time for a seed to be blown out, because fire gets rid of all the dead plant litter on the ground. Bare ground is an easier place for a seed to grow.

Two animals in the western Sierra Nevada mountains, where giant sequoias grow, open a lot of cones for the giant sequoias. One is a very active little squirrel called the chickaree. Chickarees eat the fleshy scales of sequoia cones, but they don't eat the seeds, which are very small. If the cones are eaten in the treetops, the seeds often flutter away in the wind. Chickarees sometimes cut giant sequoia cones loose with their teeth and drop them to the ground, to be hidden in the leaf litter and eaten later. One chickaree was observed to cut 538 sequoia cones in 31 minutes! As the stored cones are uncovered and eaten in winter, the uneaten seeds are scattered about so they are ready to germinate in spring. Those stored ones that are forgotten and uneaten may dry out and may release their seeds on the ground.

A very small wood-boring beetle (*Phymatodes nitidus*) also plays an important role in seed dispersal. The female beetle lays her eggs at the bases of the cone scales, where they join the central core of the cone. The tiny larvae that hatch from the eggs feed on the interior of the cone, often cutting the vascular tissue of the cone and thereby cutting off the water supply to the scales. The scales then turn brown, dry up, and shrink, creating open spaces between them. The seeds are able to slip out and blow away.

How Do They Do That?

The average age of a giant sequoia at maturity is 2,000 to 3,000 years. It's difficult to estimate the age of a living tree. We can tell its age for sure only if it is cut down. If you ever see the stump of a recently cut tree, look at the rings on the top surface of the stump. The smallest ring in the center of the stump represents the tree's first year of growth, when it was a skinny little thing. Outside of that smallest ring you will see a pattern of alternating light and dark rings. Each dark ring is one spring's growth and each light ring is one summer's growth. So if you count either the light rings or the dark rings (not both), all the way from the center to the bark, you will find the number of years that the tree has been alive. By counting rings, we know that one sequoia stump came from a tree that lived to be 3,200 to 3,300 years old.

How do they live so long? Giant sequoias and their cousins, the coast redwoods, are very resistant to insects and disease. They seldom if ever die from insect damage, disease, or old age. This is very unusual in the plant world. Many types of trees can live 200 or 300 years, but sooner or later an injury allows insects or a plant virus or a fungus to invade the tree, and it eventually dies. This can happen with animals and people, too. When we get a tear in our skin (a scrape or a cut), we can also be invaded by disease-causing organisms. Bacteria in particular. Before we had antibiotic medicines, people often died from injuries that became infected by bacteria. But today, when a cut becomes infected, we take medicines that kill the bacteria.

The bark and the heartwood of sequoias and redwoods contain a chemical called tannin that repels insects. (Heartwood is the inner wood of the trunk, as opposed to the newly formed outer sapwood.) Small mammals and birds sometimes take dust baths in powdered bark at the base of a sequoia or redwood, because the tannin in the dust repels fleas.

Many trees of various kinds are killed in forest fires. But giant sequoias and redwoods are also very resistant to fires. Their very thick bark contains no resin, a substance that is very flammable and makes other trees burn easily. If you look closely at the bark of any mature sequoia or redwood, you can probably see flecks of black in the bark. These are from fires in the distant past that scorched the surface, but did not damage the tree. Even when fires are hot enough or last long enough to damage sequoias, the trees are very seldom killed by the damage. Very old sequoias may have huge, cave-like fire scars at their base, but still appear to be perfectly healthy, with plenty of green foliage at their tops.

If sequoias and redwoods don't die from insects or disease or fire or old age, then what kills them? Redwoods are still logged extensively outside of areas such as national parks. But most mature sequoias are now protected from cutting. The most likely cause of death for a sequoia is falling over. Both sequoias and redwoods have very shallow roots, so the trees are not very well anchored. If a giant sequoia is growing at the edge of a moist meadow, the side in the moister soil may sink a bit more than the other side. This can cause the tree to lean. If it leans too much, the shallow roots can't hold it up against the pull of gravity and it will fall. Strong winds and landslides can cause a sequoia to topple, especially one that is already leaning or has a gaping fire scar on one side.

The Tallest Living Thing

Giant sequoias may be the biggest and heaviest trees, but some redwoods are taller. The tallest living redwood is 367 feet (112 m) tall. Sequoias are considered to be bigger because they are much thicker than redwoods, which makes them heavier. Many giant sequoias are greater than 30 feet (9 m) in diameter, while mature redwoods are seldom more than 20 feet (6 m).

Sequoias and coast redwoods are closely related and are very similar in many ways. Both are in the redwood family, Taxodiaceae. Like the giant sequoia, the coast redwood is a cone-bearing tree that lives in California. It grows a bit farther north than the giant sequoia and right on the Pacific coast of northern California. The best stands of redwoods are within 30 miles of the ocean, in areas that are often foggy.

The growth habits of redwoods are different from those of sequoias. Giant sequoias usually stand alone, bathed in sunshine. Their nearest neighbors are other kinds of trees that are much smaller. But redwoods grow in dense stands of other redwoods, often so close together that a person has trouble squeezing between them. They are so densely packed that they block out much of the light from above. So a redwood forest is dimly lit and foggy, with little undergrowth other than ferns.

Redwoods have reddish brown bark that may be 3 to 10 inches (8 to 25 cm) thick, and a trunk that flares out at the bottom to support its height. Their leaves are flat **needles** less than 1 inch (2.5 cm) long. The crown of the tree (the branches all together) is not round, but narrow and irregular. The cones are only ⅘ to 1 inch (2 to 2.5 cm) long, smaller than the cones of a giant sequoia.

Giant sequoias must grow from seeds. But redwoods can grow from the underground roots of a stump or from the roots of a living tree. Mature redwoods are sometimes surrounded by dozens or even hundreds of new sprouts. Redwood trees can be seen in Redwood National Park, Muir Woods National Monument, and many other sites in coastal California.

Where They Live

Giant sequoias are native to the western slopes of the southern Sierra Nevada range of California. They are found nowhere else. This is a relatively dry and cold area, where most of the precipitation is snow. Sequoias grow in fairly open areas, not in dense clusters. Nearby trees are likely to be much shorter species, such as white fir, ponderosa pine, and cedar.

Huge numbers of giant sequoias were cut down in the mid to late 1800s for lumber, when American settlers spread into California. Sometimes they were left to rot where they fell, because they turned out to be too heavy to move. Many of the remaining trees are protected now in Yosemite, Kings Canyon, and Sequoia National Parks, and in Calaveras Big Trees State Park. The largest of the living sequoias is called the General Sherman tree in Sequoia National Park. It is not necessarily the tallest sequoia, but is considered to have the greatest volume. General Sherman is 275 feet (84 m) tall, 36 feet (11 m) in diameter at its base, and weighs about 600 tons (544 metric tons). It is the largest living thing on Earth. General Grant, in the same park, is 40 feet (12.2 m) in diameter at its base, but tapers more quickly so that its total volume is less. With a height of 267 feet (81 m), it is also a little shorter.

Protecting Our Giant Trees

If you are interested in learning more about sequoias and redwoods and about efforts to protect them from logging and from land development, contact one of the following organizations:

Save-the-Redwoods League
114 Sansome Street, Room 605
San Francisco, CA 94104
Phone: 415 362-2352
www.savetheredwoods.org
E-mail: info@savetheredwoods.org

Sequoia Natural History Association
Sequoia National Park
Ash Mountain, P.O. Box 10
Three Rivers, CA 93271
Phone: 209 565-3344

Redwood Natural History Association
Redwood National Park
1111 Second Street
Crescent City, CA 95532
Phone: 707 464-9150

The Yosemite Association
P.O. Box 545
Yosemite National Park, CA 95389
Phone: 209 379-2646

Calaveras Big Tree Association
Calaveras Big Tree State Park
P.O. Box 120
Arnold, CA 95223
Phone: 209 795-2334

Santa Cruz Mountains Natural
    History Association
Santa Cruz Mountains Area
101 N. Big Trees Road
Felton, CA 95018
Phone: 408 335-3174

The Oldest Living Tree

What could be older than the oldest giant sequoia? Bristlecone pines. These are pine trees of the western United States. They live in many mountain locations, usually at elevations of 7,000 to 11,000 feet (2,100 to 3,350 m), where the air is windy and cold.

Like all pine trees, bristlecones have long, thin, green needles instead of broad, flat leaves. They have cones instead of flowers. Their cones are about 3 inches (8 cm) long. Young bristlecone pines are shaped somewhat like Christmas trees, but as they get older, their shape becomes more irregular. These trees grow very slowly. In ideal conditions, a bristlecone pine can grow to be 60 feet (18 m) tall and 1 to 2 feet (30 to 60 cm) in diameter, but most never get taller than about 35 feet (11 m).

In the Sierra Nevada range of California, in Inyo National Forest, are some very, very old bristlecone pine trees. They live at an elevation of 11,000 feet (3,350 m), surrounded by snowy mountain peaks. Conditions there are very harsh. The ground is bare and rocky, and the climate is bitterly cold. The bristlecone pines that survive there are not robust, healthy trees. They are gnarled and twisted. Large parts of them are leafless, barkless, jagged deadwood. They look like weathered driftwood you might find on a beach. But on one side you can see living bark and living green needles. And they are still firmly planted in the rocky ground, still living and growing where very little else can live.

In the 1950s, a scientist named George Schulman was able to prove that some of these bristlecone pines are over 4,000 years old. We know now that the oldest are about 4,600 years old. These oldest bristlecone pines began life about the time that the first Egyptian pyramids were built. They were already 2,000 years old when the very first European civilizations appeared—Greece and Rome. They were almost 3,000 years old when the first civilizations in North and South America developed!

bristlecone
pine

Mangroves

That's Strange!

Imagine that you are a Native American child living in southern Florida, before the Europeans came to this continent. Your mother has sent you to gather food for your family for the evening meal. She doesn't say where to go or what to get, but you know where you want to go. You pick up a paddle and ask your mom for a basket. While she isn't looking, you grab your older brother's spear and dash out the door. At the edge of the village you lift one of the small canoes onto your back. After a few minutes' walk, you arrive at the salt marsh. With the basket and spear at your feet, you paddle silently into the marsh, toward the wide expanse of mangrove trees in the water. How different they are from other trees, you think, with their long, curved roots sticking so far up into the air. You could live inside that tangle of roots if you had to, and never come out. Your canoe enters the silence and shade of the mangrove canopy. You're glad your canoe is small enough to fit through these narrow passageways. You paddle a bit farther, and you see mussels within reach, on roots just below the surface. With effort, you manage to break off several and toss them into the basket. Then off to the side you spot a couple of big snails. They'll be good, your mother will be pleased at that. You easily pluck them from the root and add them to the basket. There's a crab up out of the water! You hold the basket under it and knock it in with the end of the spear. You glide on, trying not to bump the branches. A bird's nest! You know that some hunters would take the eggs, but you decide to leave them. The birds are your friends, even now their calls keep you company. Just one more crab or a couple more snails, and that will be enough.

mangrove swamp

You hear your name called from the edge of the marsh. It's your older brother. He wants his spear back. He's calling you names, insulting your skills as a hunter. He says he's going to pound you for taking his spear. But he'll never find you in here. You could be anywhere in the mangroves. Maybe you can get something big with that spear yet, and show him who knows about hunting. You hear a branch break up ahead where the water gets very shallow. Maybe a raccoon or a fox! You'll show that brother. But it's not a raccoon. It's a panther! And it's looking right at you, stepping silently toward you! Your stomach jumps and your heart pounds wildly. Your arms tremble and shake as you try to back the canoe out. Suddenly the mangroves are all in your way. You scream in panic, wildly flailing the paddle all around at the trees. The panther turns and runs. And all at once, there is your brother at your side. "Whoa, little one, calm down," he says. "The panther is gone. Let me get into the canoe with you. We'll paddle on together, and I'll show you how to spear a big fish for Mama. Won't she be surprised?"

What They Look Like   Mangroves are shrubs or small trees that grow in coastal areas, in shallow salt water or a mixture of fresh- and salt water. They can grow as tall as 50 to 80 feet under ideal conditions, but are usually much shorter. Their leaves are oval and leathery. The trees are considered to be evergreen, which means that they don't shed their leaves in fall as maples and hickories and many other trees do. Rather, they keep their leaves all year around, as pine trees keep their needles. The flowers on a mangrove tree are small and light yellow.

Mangroves are very odd looking because they have roots that grow down from the branches. The roots pass through air and water and into the mud or sand beneath the tree. They look like arching and branching stilts all around the tree. They support the tree in the loose, wet soil. Roots like these are called **aerial roots** because they grow through air. They are also called **prop roots** because they prop up the tree. A few other kinds of trees have aerial roots, such as the strangler figs and banyan trees described in the final chapter.

Tropical shores are often covered with mangroves. The trees grow close together so that the prop roots of one tree grow right next to the roots of its neighbor. An area of mangroves can look like a vast, leafy jungle gym, stretching in both directions as far as the eye can see.

mangrove plant

How Do They Do That?

Most plants can't survive in salt water or salty soil. Salt draws the water out of living things. People can swim in salt water because our skin is waterproof, but we can't drink much of it without getting sick. Animals, algae, and one-celled organisms that live in salt water have special ways of dealing with the salt. But very, very few flowering plants can tolerate a salty environment.

So how do mangroves live in salt water? Different species of mangroves have different solutions. Red mangroves have waterproof membranes that keep most salt from entering their roots. White mangroves and black mangroves let in more salt, but then they excrete it through little glands on the leaves. You may be able to see salt crystals on the leaves. Rain washes the crystals away.

Mangroves have another problem that they've had to overcome in order to live where they do. Most plants take in oxygen through their roots. Plants need oxygen for the same reason we do—oxygen is part of the reaction that breaks down food for energy. But the soil or mud where mangroves live has little or no oxygen in it. The soil is often a thick liquid muck rather than solid land. If you stepped on it, you might sink up past your ankles. When you pulled your feet out, you would smell the rotten-egg odor of swamp gas. That smell means that the soil contains lots of nutrients, lots of decaying plant and animal matter, but no oxygen.

So how do mangroves get oxygen? They have special pores or small openings above water called lenticels that let oxygen in. White mangroves have lenticels on their trunks. Red mangroves have lenticels on their prop roots. Some mangroves have lenticels on special fingerlike knobs that stick up out of the muck.

Mangroves can grow quite well without salt water, and even on dry land. Then why do we find them almost always growing in shallow salt water? Because they have no competition there. Other plants that shade them out and crowd them out on land cannot survive in salt water.

Since mangroves are flowering plants, they must have seeds. After their small, yellow flowers are pollinated, each flower produces a small, brown fruit. Each fruit contains one seed. Mangrove seeds would be killed by salt water, so they can't just drop off in the salt water and float away. Instead, the

mangrove seedling still on parent tree

mangrove seedling taking root

seeds sprout into young plants while they're still on the parent tree. Each seedling has a thick root, which may grow more than a foot long while still attached to Mom. Although the seed could not survive in salt water, the seedling can. When it finally drops off, it floats away. The seedling, sometimes called a propagule, may travel around for months on ocean currents, with its stem in the air and its root underwater. If it floats into a shallow area where the root bumps the ground, then smaller roots will begin to grow and will snag the ground. Soon the seedling is anchored in the muck and it begins to grow into a mangrove tree.

Areas with lots of mangrove trees are called mangrove swamps. These swamps provide **habitats** (natural homes) for thousands of creatures, both above water and underwater. Not only do the mangroves provide home and shelter, they also provide food. The mangrove food web (who eats whom) starts with the tons of leaves that each acre of mangroves drops into the water each year. When the leaves fall into the water one by one, they are broken into pieces by crabs, other crustaceans, and snails. The tiny bits of leaves are eaten by bacteria, crustaceans, worms, small fish, and other small animals. One-celled organisms and sponges eat the bacteria. Microscopic animals called **plankton** eat the one-celled organisms. Barnacles, oysters, and mussels on the prop roots feed on the plankton and on tiny particles suspended in the water. Small fish eat all of these things. Larger fish eat the small fish. Many deepwater fish spend their youth in the relative shelter of mangroves, moving out to sea as they get older. There they become food for other ocean animals and for birds.

The algae that grows on the prop roots is eaten by snails and other creatures. Crabs and lobsters crawl across the mud and hang out in the prop roots, eating whatever they can.

Above water, the mangrove is home to more animals—the mangrove crab, lizards, spiders, hundreds of insect species, and more snails. Rodents, skunks, raccoons, river otters, and bobcats look for food among the mangroves.

Birds are probably the most noticeable users of the mangroves. The trees offer everything that many birds need for feeding, resting, and nesting. Long-legged shorebirds poke their long, slim bills into the mud or sand looking for small creatures. Herons, egrets, and ibises walk through the water on their stilt legs, striking at fish. Kingfishers, cormorants, and pelicans dive into the water for fish. Roseate spoonbills (tall, pink birds) filter tiny creatures from the water with their spoon-shaped bills.

Humans, too, have learned to partake of the rich and productive mangrove food web. We harvest shrimp (a type of crustacean) from the mangroves—about a ton of shrimp for each 60 acres of mangroves each year. We harvest many species of fish that either feed in the mangroves or spend their young lives there. Unfortunately, we harvest so many fish that we don't leave enough behind for the birds of the mangroves. Some have declined in number because their nestlings starve.

Mangroves and 181 Bird Species

Three scientists (William E. Odum, Carole C. McIvor, and Thomas J. Smith) studied the mangrove swamps of southern Florida and reported on the number of birds using mangroves during a single year. They found that 181 species of birds used the mangroves at one time or another during the year. Sixty-six bird species nested there. Several species of large and beautiful birds of southern Florida nest only in mangroves—roseate spoonbills, brown pelicans, reddish egrets, and great white herons. Many others nest mostly in mangroves and still others, such as bald eagles, ospreys, and peregrine falcons, are dependent on the mangroves for their survival in southern Florida. These birds of prey feed on animals from the mangrove food chain. Osprey feed on fish, falcons on birds, and eagles on both.

Where They Live

Mangroves grow along saltwater coasts in shallow water. They grow in coastal swamps, bays, tidal creeks, and **estuaries** (where a freshwater river meets the ocean). Since coastal water levels rise and fall with daily ocean tides, mangrove roots may be entirely out of water for periods of each day.

Mangroves are found all around the world, but only in tropical and semitropical climates. These climates occur in countries that are relatively close to the equator. In the United States, mangroves are plentiful in southern Florida. Some mangrove trees live out of water in the city of Miami. Mangroves also grow along the coast of the Gulf of Mexico, in Florida, Alabama, Mississippi, Louisiana, and Texas.

What You Can See and Do

If you are fortunate enough to visit a southern coast or saltwater marsh, you can recognize mangroves by their stiltlike prop roots. Use a bird field guide to identify some of the birds flying in and out of the mangroves. You may see a heron or an egret. Early morning is probably the best time to look. If you are with an adult who has a canoe or a rowboat, have him or her take you in among the prop roots. Look carefully at the surface of the roots. You might see the pores, or lenticels, where oxygen passes into the roots. Look carefully for insects, lizards, birds, and any other creatures above the water. Do you see mangrove crabs perching on the roots? Underwater you may see algae, oysters, mussels, barnacles, worms, and more crabs on the prop roots. You will probably hear the whine of mosquitoes, so wear insect repellent!

━━━◄ Mangroves in Peril ►━━━

All around the world, mangroves and their food webs are in danger. Overfishing of mangrove areas is a problem worldwide. In developing countries, such as in Central America and Asia, people often cut the trees for wood. Mangrove swamps are often cleared and filled with dry soil to provide space for building houses or other structures. Of course, swamps that are filled never recover. Sadly, mangrove swamps that are simply cleared and then left alone usually don't recover either, for a number of reasons. Mangrove seedlings grow much better in the shade of other mangroves. When exposed to full sunlight, they grow very slowly. Water currents are likely to carry away the nutrient-rich muck where mangroves have been removed, leaving a hard bottom that mangrove seedlings can't hold on to. A faster growing shrub, such as saltwort, may take over a cleared area.

We have lots of reasons to care what happens to mangroves. A mangrove swamp is one of the richest **ecosystems** (natural communities) in the world. An ecosystem is a group of living things that depend on one another. The mangrove trees support a fantastic array of living things that cannot survive without them. A number of connections may not be obvious, such as oceanic birds that feed on deep-sea fish. Although these fish may be eaten far from the coast, they may have grown up in a mangrove swamp. Mangroves are important to endangered species, too. The mangroves of Florida alone support seven endangered species, including Atlantic ridley sea turtles, crocodiles, and Florida panthers.

Another reason to care is that we harvest so many creatures from mangroves—shrimp, lobsters, fish—for our own food. If we don't take care to protect these animals and their habitat worldwide, we'll soon find that both animals and habitat have disappeared.

Orchids

That's Strange!

The male wasp is looking for a female. When he finds her, they will mate and then she will lay eggs. She will need several meals of flower nectar before she lays the eggs. The sugary nectar provides the energy she needs to produce the eggs and to lay them. But the females of this wasp subfamily (Thyninae) have no wings. So the male must carry the female from flower to flower, to find the nectar she needs for egg laying.

male thynnid wasp being fooled by the *Drakaea* orchid

The male finds the female by following her special scent in the air. She produces the scent as a signal to the male. It tells him that a female of his species is available for mating. (A scent that has a social message like this is called a **pheromone**.) A male wasp can't see details nearly as well as we can, but when he finds the source of the powerful scent, he recognizes her general shape, her texture, and her color. He flies to her, lands on her back, beats his wings with all his might, and lifts her into the air. They mate in the air, then he carries her from flower to flower so that she can get the nectar she needs.

This arrangement works very smoothly for the wasp couple, except when the male is scammed and slammed by an orchid! Sometimes he flies to that attractive female scent, spots a female and lands on her, beats his wings . . . and gets smacked up against the male part of an orchid flower! He's been tricked! One of the petals of a *Drakaea* orchid has developed into a form that looks and feels like the wingless body of a female wasp. More importantly, the orchid has produced the important pheromone. The scent tells the male that a female of his species is here.

Look, Don't Pick

If you are fortunate enough to spot a lady's slipper or any other orchid growing outdoors, enjoy it where it is. Don't pick it and don't dig it up to move to your garden. In some states it is illegal to pick or move a lady's slipper. These and all orchids are very finicky about their growing conditions and will almost certainly die sooner or later if moved. In nature they can live for many years. They will also have many descendants over many years in nature. When someone removes a flower from the wild, they remove all or many of its descendants as well. Many orchid species around the world are in trouble because of overcollecting.

Orchids are expensive and tricky to take care of. If you are interested in buying one anyway, don't get one that was taken from nature. Make sure that it was raised in a greenhouse. Ask for instructions about its care, and follow them carefully. If and when your plant flowers, the flower may last for months.

The family of orchids, Orchidaceae, is the largest or one of the largest families of plants. Estimates of the number of species vary from 18,000 to 35,000. There is a tremendous amount of variation among these orchid species. But, in general, orchids are considered among the most beautiful flowers in the world. The flowers are often several inches across, with bright colors and vivid patterns. A single blossom may have several different colors on it.

Many people breed and grow orchids as a hobby or as a business. You can buy an orchid as a potted plant or in a **corsage** to pin on a dress or a suit for a dance or a fancy night out. Orchids are very hard to grow in gardens or containers, so you don't see them everywhere. Because they are hard to grow and because they are so beautiful, they are very expensive.

Many species of orchids are so closely related that you can fertilize the eggs of one species with the pollen of another species. This doesn't happen very often in nature, but people who grow orchids as a hobby or business often do it by hand. They collect pollen from one species and put it on the female part, or pistil, of another species. If seeds are produced by this female flower part, then the seed will grow into a new **variety** of orchid that has characteristics of each parent species. The flower may have new shades of color or new shapes not seen before. In this way, orchid lovers are continually trying to make new varieties of orchids. A new and beautiful variety may sell for a lot of money.

Most orchids are tropical or subtropical species that grow as epiphytes. This means that they grow on the branches of rain forest trees, especially in cloud forests. Their roots cling to the bark of their host trees, but they are not parasites, like mistletoe, rafflesia, and the underground orchid *Rhizanthella* are. They don't steal the food of the host tree. Rather, they get their nourishment from water dripping off overhead plants, and from dead plant and animal matter stuck in the cracks of the tree's bark. They also have green leaves that are able to make sugars through photosynthesis. Living as an epiphyte puts them closer to the top of the forest, where sunlight is available for photosynthesis. In a rain forest, very little sunlight reaches the forest floor. It is blocked by the leaves of the treetops, or canopy. Epiphytes flourish in the moist, warm environment of a tropical rain forest. Here, their roots are safe from freezing, and water is abundant.

Orchids that grow in cooler places cannot be epiphytes, because their roots would freeze during a cold winter. So orchids in cooler places are rooted in the ground. Soil protects roots from freezing air temperatures.

Although there is a lot of variation in the orchid family, there are a few characteristics that apply to most orchids. For one thing, the male and female parts of orchid flowers have an unusual arrangement. Most types of flowers have a female organ called a pistil in the center of the flower, and male organs, on stalks and bearing pollen, are arranged in a circle around the pistil. But in an orchid flower, the male and female organs are side by side on one structure called a **column.** The orchid flower still has a pistil and at least one male organ, but they are fused together.

Another distinctive trait of orchids is the packaging of the pollen. In an orchid flower, the grains of pollen from the male organ are stuck together in club-shaped bundles called **pollinia** (singular **pollinium**). When an insect carries pollen from one flower to another, it carries the whole bundle, or usually two bundles.

Another oddity of orchids is that one petal on each flower is different from the other petals. This odd petal is called the **lip** or **labellum.** It is often folded to make round or hollow or intricate shapes. If the flower is hanging or leaning, the lip is usually on the lower side of the flower. Often the lip has a role in attracting or trapping insects that will carry away or bring pollen for the orchid.

Orchids of the genera *Drakaea, Caladenia,* and *Chiloglottis* all have a lip that resembles a wingless female wasp, as described in the first paragraphs of this chapter. Even more famous for their trickery are the orchids of the genus *Ophrys.* This genus has about 30 species in Europe, Asia, and North Africa. The bee orchid, the bumblebee orchid, and many other *Ophrys* species have a flower with an oval-shaped, fuzzy, brown labellum, like the fuzzy, brown bodies of the bees they attract. They look and feel like female bees to the males. And like the wingless wasp orchids, *Ophrys* blossoms produce the sexual scents of the female bees that they resemble. The male bees find these mimics irresistible.

Ophrys or bee orchid

Why Do They Do That?

Why would an orchid flower lure a male wasp, by pretending to be a female wasp? When the male wasp beats his wings hard, he lifts the fake "female," which is really the labellum, or odd petal, of the orchid flower. But the labellum, like all petals, is attached at one end to the flower. So his effort lifts only the rear part of his body. His head is tipped down and his back is whacked hard against the column, the central part of the flower. When this happens, the pollinia, or pollen bundles, become attached to his back. The flower has lured and tricked him so that he will carry these pollinia on, to another flower of the same species. The next time he is tricked and thrown up against the column of an orchid, some of the pollinia will come off. Some will come to rest on the female part of this flower, and will fertilize its eggs so that they can form seeds. So while the male wasp is trying to find a mate for himself, he is really helping the orchid flowers to mate.

This kind of trickery and deceit occurs in many different species of orchids. The orchid family is famous for its artful designs that lure and trap insects. Secret passages, snapping hinges, slippery surfaces. It's all for the sake of pollination. Like many other plant families, orchids depend on insects to carry pollen from the male part of one flower to the female part of another flower. When roses or daisies or most other common garden flowers attract insects, there is no trickery involved. The flower advertises with its scent and its colors that nectar is available. Bees, wasps, and other insects come to get the nectar, and as they feed, a few pollen grains stick to their bodies. At the next flower, a few pollen grains come off. It's quite simple. So why do orchids resort to trickery? One reason may be that the pollinia produced by an orchid are much bigger and heavier than the dusting of pollen grains a bee gets when it visits a rose. Sticking heavy and bulky pollinia to a visiting insect requires some force. But the pollinia, when they are delivered, carry thousands of grains of pollen. One pollinium can fertilize all the eggs in a flower at once.

The orchids that imitate female insects are fascinating, but the orchids with traps are just as complex, or more so. While a bee is visiting one of these orchids, it becomes temporarily trapped by some structure in the flower. Each trap has only one exit. As the bee moves through the exit, it either picks up pollinia from the flower, or delivers pollinia that it has carried from another flower.

A couple of very famous groups of orchids that have traps are the common lady's slippers of North America and the bucket orchids of Latin America. There are many species of both. On a bucket orchid, part of the labellum is shaped like a bucket. Certain male bees are attracted to bucket orchids by powerful scents. They are **euglossine bees,** or orchid bees. Scientists have found that these bees will flock to the scent even if it is just smeared on a paper towel.

The scent is available to the bees in the form of tiny wax droplets. One bucket orchid that has been studied carefully is *Coryanthes speciosa.* Its scented wax is on a vertical stalk that attaches to the top of the bucket like the handle on a soup ladle. The stalk connects the bucket to the rest of the flower. The bees crawl around on the slippery stalk

vertical stalk

Coryanthes speciosa, **a bucket orchid**

and collect the scented wax with their legs. They tuck it into pockets on their hind legs. Why do the male bees collect and store the scent? It is thought that the males change the scents somehow and then use the new scents to attract females. There may be a lot of excited bees on the stalk at once. A bee may get knocked off the stalk. It falls into a shallow liquid inside the bucket. The sides of the bucket are slippery and the soggy bee can't crawl up. But there is a way out. The bee finds a foothold, and over that, one opening in the side of the bucket. The opening is a short, tight tunnel. On the roof of the tunnel are portions of the male and female organs of the flower. As the bee squeezes past them, two pollinia stick to its back. If it already has pollinia on its back when it enters the tunnel, then a sort of hook in the tunnel pulls off the two bundles that it has, fertilizing the female part of the orchid. It may take the bee 45 minutes to wiggle its way through the tunnel!

lady's slipper

The lady's slipper is a more familiar orchid that also has a trap. It also has a lip that forms a sort of bucket. But in this case, the bucket looks a bit like a slipper—a shoe with no laces or buckles. The slipper hangs down, so the "toe" is toward the ground and a large opening is at the top. Bees are attracted by color (often pink or yellow) and by a scent that suggests nectar. A bee enters through a small opening near the toe. There is no liquid in the slipper. But there are folds inside that keep the insect from leaving the way it came in. The bee is attracted to the light at the top of the slipper and moves toward the opening there. Some lady's slippers have nectar-covered hairs that guide the bee toward the top; others cheat the bee and provide no nectar. When the bee leaves through the top opening of the slipper, it is forced to drag its back across the female and male orchid parts, which are hanging just above the exit. If it already has pollinia on its back, it leaves them on the female part. And it picks up pollinia from the male part, for the next flower.

In the chapters on carnivorous plants, you learned that pitcher plants, sundews, and others trap and kill insects for food. Orchids don't hurt or kill the insects they trap. They release them unharmed, so that the insects can fly on and deliver any pollen that has been picked up.

Where They Live

Orchids live on every continent, except Antarctica. They are found from the arctic tundra to the equator. Some live on cold mountain tops, others in low-land swampy areas. The majority are found in the tropical or subtropical areas of the world, especially South America, Madagascar, and the islands around Malaysia. Most of these are epiphytes, many with large, colorful flowers. There are about 285 species of wild orchids in the United States and Canada. Most of these are rooted orchids with small flowers, such as the many species of lady's slippers. Some of the subtropical species of orchids that are epiphytes can be found in Florida and southern California.

The Christmas Star

In the 1800s, a beautiful white orchid was discovered in Madagascar. Its starlike flowers measured almost 7 inches (18 cm) across. The sweet-smelling orchid bloomed around Christmas, and so it was called the star of Bethlehem, or Christmas star.

This dazzling flower had one feature that puzzled scientists of the time. Its nectar was at the bottom of a very narrow, almost 12-inch-long (30 cm) tube hanging from the flower. Such a tube was much too long for any known insect or bird to be able to reach the nectar. The only reason flowers of any kind produce nectar is to attract insects or other animals. When animals come to drink nectar, they often pick up pollen on their bodies and carry it on to the female structure of the next flower. Pollinators that drink nectar are usually bees, wasps, butterflies, moths, or hummingbirds. But who could get to the bottom of a 12-inch-long (30 cm) tube as thin as a thread?

Charles Darwin, the famous scientist who first figured out and explained evolution, decided that the pollinator who was coming for the nectar had to be an insect, probably a moth with a 10- or 11-inch (25 to 28 cm) tongue! But no such insect was known. Other scientists scoffed at him. They said he only suggested such a ridiculous notion in order to support his idea that plants and animals sometimes change and evolve to fit each other's needs. Ha! said the other scientists. What animal could have a thread-thin body part that could reach that far?

About 40 years later, a moth was discovered on the island of Madagascar with an 11-inch (28 cm) tongue. It was given the subspecies name *praedicta*, because it fulfilled Charles Darwin's prediction. When this moth presses its face into the Christmas star to reach the nectar, it picks up the flower's pollinia on its tongue and eyes. It delivers the little packets to the next Christmas star it visits.

Darwin was fascinated by the traps and tricks orchids have evolved to make use of pollinating insects. He wrote a two-volume book *The Various Contrivances by Which Orchids Are Fertilized by Insects,* which is regarded by scientists as a classic.

Saguaro Cactus

That's Strange!

What a convenient place to live. It has plenty of space and a twenty-four hour cafeteria. A great view. It's historic, too—over 200 years old. This apartment building is so popular that its tenants are often disturbed by others checking for a vacancy. "Anyone home? Oh, excuse me, I didn't realize this apartment was occupied. I'll look somewhere else." It's a very busy place. Some residents are in and out all night long. Others are in and out all day long. Must be hard for anyone to get a wink of sleep. But no one's complaining. It's a great place for desert living. Cool in the daytime, warm at night, dry and secure, with barbed wire all the way to the ground. No need to worry about intruders here. Yep, it's a good life as a resident of a great saguaro cactus. The giant cactus is

saguaros and their visitors

home to many different animals in the Sonoran Desert of Arizona. Without it, many of them wouldn't be able to survive the desert's harsh environment.

What They Look Like

A saguaro cactus begins life as a black seed no bigger than a pinhead. It won't sprout unless it lands in the shade of a scrubby desert tree or bush. Then it grows very slowly. After a year it is no bigger than a pencil eraser. After 15 years, it is still only as tall as a bowling pin. After 25 years, it is as tall as a yardstick, and still growing. At first the little cactus is round like a ball. But as it gets taller, it takes on the shape of a pole or column. Between the ages of 50 and 60, the cactus grows its first branch. It will grow many more branches as it gets older. The branches grow upward, so that a mature saguaro looks like a candelabra, a candlestick with branches for many candles. The saguaro may live as long as 200 or even 300 years. It may grow as tall as a telephone pole, or even as tall as a four-story building! An area with many saguaros is sometimes called a saguaro forest.

Like all cactuses, saguaros have sharp, pointed spines instead of leaves. The trunk, branches, and spines are green. In most plants, photosynthesis occurs in the cells of the leaves. But since a cactus has no leaves, it carries out photo-

saguaro

synthesis in the surface cells of the trunk and branches instead. Through photosynthesis, cactuses and all other green plants use the energy of the sun to make sugar.

A saguaro cactus has pleats like an accordion on its outer surface. Ridges and deep grooves run from the top of the plant to the bottom, on all sides. The outer skin is tough, but the tissue underneath the skin is softer. After the rainy season, this tissue is almost as soft as the fruit of a watermelon.

Because it is so heavy and so tall, a saguaro has several strong woody rods inside the trunk. The rods are long and thin, like bamboo. These vertical rods support the weight of the cactus, and keep it from blowing over.

saguaro flowers and flower buds

In spring, dozens of flower buds form on the top of the trunk and on the top of each branch. They open at night into creamy white flowers that are 2 inches (5.1 cm) across and 4 inches (10.2 cm) deep. Each flower opens for only one night. After the flowers are pollinated, they develop into green fruits full of seeds. The fruits turn red as they ripen. Clusters of the sweet and juicy fruits cover the end of each branch and trunk.

Why Do They Do That?

Saguaros live in the desert, where there is very little rainfall. Yet, like all living things, saguaros need water to live. How does such a big plant survive and thrive in such a parched place?

Saguaros have a number of water-saving adaptations that most plants don't have. First of all, they have no leaves. Most leaves lose water continually, in the form of water vapor. A large tree can lose 100 gallons of water in a single day through its leaves! Saguaros have spines instead of leaves. Spines don't lose water, and they also protect the plant from some of the animals that might eat it or try to get water from it.

You might think that a saguaro could lose water through its green trunk, since it has almost no bark. But the trunk has a thick and waxy skin that keeps water in.

Saguaros are good at hanging on to the water they have. They are good at storing water, too. In the Sonoran Desert, there are two rainy seasons each year, in late winter and midsummer. During these rainy spells, a saguaro absorbs water with its roots. The water is stored in the trunk. The tissue in the trunk swells with water until the vertical grooves in the trunk almost flatten out. The ridges move farther apart and the diameter of the trunk may increase by 20 percent. Sometimes the trunk may keep swelling until its skin splits! The saguaro can store enough water to last for at least 3 years.

Many animals visit or live in giant saguaros. These giant cactuses are by far the tallest plant in the desert where they live. There are a few hardy bushes and trees in the area, but they are very short. Hawks often rest at the top of a saguaro. From there, they can watch for small mammals, birds, and lizards to eat. If a favorite perch at the top of a saguaro is already occupied, a hawk may perch on the back of another hawk. In fact, a third hawk may land on the back of the second one!

Although the saguaro is almost covered with spines, it can make a good place for nesting, too. Harris' hawks, great horned owls, and ospreys build nests on the branches, where the branches leave the trunk. Woodpeckers and owls nest inside the trunks of saguaros. Gilded flickers (a type of woodpecker) and gila woodpeckers use their bills to dig out a deep hole in the side of a saguaro's trunk. The spines don't seem to bother them. Gila woodpeckers break off the sharp points of the spines around the hole. The outer skin of a saguaro is tough, but the digging occurs shortly after the late winter rains, when the cactus flesh under the surface is waterlogged and soft. A pair of gila woodpeckers dig a hole in the saguaro that goes straight back about 6 or 7 inches (15 to 17 cm). Then they dig down about 14 inches (35.5 cm), forming a room inside the cactus about the size of a football. The cactus oozes juices from the spongy tissues as the woodpeckers work. These juices on the inner surfaces of the chamber harden into a stiff wall or shell. Then the room is a snug, dry place for the woodpeckers to make a soft nest and raise their young. The spongy tissue around the chamber makes great insulation. The

Harris' hawk

little room stays cool in the heat of the day. At night, when the desert cools, the air in the chamber stays warm. So the baby woodpeckers inside are protected from extreme heat and from cold. The saguaro makes a great grocery as well as a nursery. The parent woodpeckers hunt for insects under the spines of the saguaro, where there is a bit of shade from the brutal midday sun. They hunt in the vertical grooves on the trunk, a good place for crevice-loving bugs. And they hunt in and among the flower buds on top, which haven't yet opened at the time the woodpeckers are nesting.

From time to time, the woodpecker family has strange visitors. In late April or early May, elf owls arrive from warmer southern areas, looking for empty nest holes. They don't dig their own holes, but use the abandoned holes of flickers or gila woodpeckers from previous years. These tiny owls fly around from hole to hole, peeking in to see if anyone is home. When they find an empty one, they climb in and build their own nest.

Elf owls are the smallest owls in the world. They are only 5 or 6 inches (12.7 to 15.2 cm) tall, with a wingspan of 15 inches (38 cm). They are active mainly at dawn and dusk, sleeping through the heat of the day. Elf owls that nest in saguaros feed insects to their young. The adults may hang upside down from the tall flower stalk of a yucca plant, grabbing bugs from the underside of the flowers. They ignore the stinging wasps and bees, but take moths, beetles, scorpions, and centipedes. They also collect grasshoppers, crickets, and caterpillars. Scorpions can give a painful and dangerous sting with their tail, but the parent elf owls mangle the tail before delivering the scorpion to the young.

In early July, the young owls are big enough to perch in the opening of the nesting chamber in the evening. They make a rhythmic hissing sound, telling their parents that they're hungry. The tiny owls' feathers blend perfectly with the scars around the opening of the cactus.

Small owls called screech owls sometimes nest in old woodpecker holes in saguaros, too. Mice may nest there as well. The mice can climb up the saguaro easily. A single cactus may have woodpecker nest holes all up and down its length, many filled with animals seeking shelter from heat, cold, and **predators** (bigger animals that might eat them).

Other animals depend on the saguaro not for a home but for food. Long-nosed bats, white winged doves, hummingbirds, and many insects drink nectar from the white flowers. The fruits are food for others, such as foxes, coyotes, peccaries (small wild pigs), birds, and insects. Native Americans still collect the fruit to make jams, candies, and drinks. Mice, ants, and other animals eat seeds that come from the fruits. When a saguaro has died, it still provides a home and food to many animals, just as rotting logs do. Termites, beetles, hover flies, fruit flies, and many other insects feed on the decomposing cactus flesh. Small snakes, lizards, scorpions, centipedes, and other little predators crawl over and through a downed cactus, looking for insect prey.

Saguaros are a very important plant for the animals that live in the Sonoran Desert. They are so important that without them, a large part of the desert community would die out. A species that is essential to the survival of a particular community of living things is called a **keystone species.** Not all communities have a keystone species. But many do. The coconut palm tree is a keystone species on many small islands in the Pacific Ocean. The giant kelp beds in the ocean off the West Coast of the United States are, too. Mangrove trees that live in mangrove swamps are a keystone species. The starfish *Pisaster* that lives on rocks in the ocean tides off Washington State is a keystone species for the community of organisms that live on those rocks. Many experiments have shown that when *Pisaster* is removed, the number of other species in the community drops drastically.

We've lost many of our saguaro "forests" to development. Deserts are turned into subdivisions for our growing human population. We need to make sure that our remaining saguaro areas are protected from development so that the elf owls and other residents of the desert will still be around for future generations.

Hi Dad, Hi Mom, Hi Dad!

Harris' hawks are handsome, dark-brown hawks with chestnut patches on the legs and shoulders, and chestnut underwings. They live in the southwestern United States. These hawks are known for their very unusual breeding habits. They often form threesomes for nest building, mating, and raising young. The threesomes may be two dads and one mom, or two moms and one dad. Harris' hawks sometimes even form groups of four parents with a single nest—two moms and two dads. Both dads mate with both moms. The two moms lay eggs in the same nest, and all four adults work together to raise the young! This is a very uncommon situation in nature. Why do they do it? Research has shown that nests attended by several adults produce more healthy young hawks than nests with only two adults. The adult hawks often hunt together. In a group, they can quickly catch and kill a large cottontail rabbit to feed the babies.

The parents in Harris' hawk nests with only one mom and one dad may still get help feeding the nestlings, even if there is no third parent. Mom and dad may get help from the grown-up offspring of the year before. These young adults are just helping out the family and practicing their skills as food gatherers. They'll need the practice the following year when they become parents themselves.

All this practice and group nesting among Harris' hawks suggests that raising nestlings must be a pretty difficult business for hawks in the hot, cold, and dry desert.

Where They Live

Saguaro cactuses live only in the Sonoran Desert. This desert is in southern Arizona and northern Mexico. Cactuses as a group live only in North and South America. There are no cactuses in any other parts of the world, except those that have been transplanted by humans.

What You Can See and Do

If you visit the Saguaro National Park of Arizona, you will see lots of saguaro cactuses and the desert community where they live. Count how many different kinds of creatures you see in the desert. If you are very quiet and move slowly, you will see more. Don't forget to look for tiny insects and soaring birds overhead. Maybe you will see Harris' hawks stacked three deep on top of a giant saguaro!

Take pictures, but don't take any young cactuses. Many kinds of cactuses are in danger because people dig them up and take them home to become house- or garden plants, or to sell in stores.

If you visit the desert in spring, try to see it once at night. When the white flowers on the saguaros open after dark, you can see the many animals that visit the flowers for nectar and carry pollen from flower to flower. Look especially for the long-nosed bats and the white-winged doves. If you are there on an evening in July, listen for the rhythmic hissing of the baby elf owls perched in their doorways. They are calling for mom and dad to hurry up with the next beakful of insects.

For more information about saguaros, contact:

Arizona-Sonora Desert Museum
2021 N. Kinney Road
Tucson, AZ 85743-8918
Phone: 520 883-1380
www.desertmuseum.org

Saguaro National Park Visitor Center
3693 South Old Spanish Trail
Tucson, AZ 85730-5601
Phone: 520 733-5153/5158
E-mail: SAGU_Administration@nps.gov

The National Park Service Web site, www.nps.gov, has links to information about each park, including Saguaro National Park.

Part III

Strange Plants That You Probably Won't Find

Giant Amazon Water Lilies

That's Strange!

You may have seen a frog perched on a lily pad floating in a pond. But have you ever seen a policeman on a lily pad? A small horse on a lily pad? A 7-year-old fairy queen on a lily pad? Probably not. Yet there is a lily pad that can and has supported all of these things. The 6-foot-wide giant Amazon water lily has been shown to support up to 300 pounds! It's so strong that its support system was copied by Joseph Paxton when he designed the Crystal Palace, a huge glass building in London's Kew Gardens, in the 1850s. No one believed Paxton's design could hold up so much glass, but it did. The Crystal Palace still stands today, as the largest glass structure in the world. Paxton also dressed his 7-year-old daughter Annie as a fairy queen and photographed her on a giant Amazon lily pad that was growing in a special pool in England. He wanted to show the world what his beloved giant water lily could do.

giant lily pad
holds up a
fairy queen

Why Do They Do That?

Why do giant Amazon water lilies grow where they do, and why do they grow so large? First, a plant in water is never in danger of drying out. The earliest plants all lived in water. Those that live there now do so because they are able to beat out their competitors in the race for space, or because they have good defenses against aquatic animals that eat plants. The Amazon water lily's size helps it in both regards.

Second, the rivers that are home to the Amazon water lilies provide not only water, but also food. Tropical rivers contain plenty of nutrients that have run into the water from the surrounding land. The river bottom is also rich in nutrients. In order for their roots to reach the mud on the river bottom, the Amazon lilies' stems may have to grow to 35 feet (10.7 m) in length!

Third, getting enough light can be a challenge for plants in water, especially in the tropics where there are so many tall trees. The easiest way for water plants to get light is to float on the surface. The more they spread out, the more light they can collect. The short, vertical rim around the edge of a giant lily pad is very good at shoving other plants out of the way as the leaf expands. The leaf may enlarge at a rate of 1 inch (2.5 cm) per hour, so it does a lot of shoving! One Amazon water lily plant can grow 40 to 50 leaves in a single season, and can fill most of the available space so that competitors are squeezed out.

What They Look Like The leaf of a giant water lily is much larger than the usual lily pad. It's about 6 feet across at maturity! Like other lily pads, it floats on the surface of the water. The leaf lies flat, but its surface is covered by small, very low mounds. The edge of the leaf is turned up to make a neat rim about 6 inches high. One early explorer of South America wrote that the leaves looked like big green tea trays.

On the purple undersurface of the leaf are ribs and struts that support its great size. It also has many air pockets on the undersurface to help it float. The undersurface is covered with sharp spikes as well. The spikes may keep fish from nibbling on it. If the leaf is removed from the water, it becomes limp and loses its shape.

The flower **bud** of a giant Amazon water lily is as large as a person's head or a head of cabbage. The flower does not develop on the leaf, but grows at the surface of the water, near the leaf. Both leaf and flower are connected by stems to a root system that draws minerals and nutrients from the mud at the bottom of the river or lake.

The flower opens for the first time in the evening. When open, it is about 15 inches across. It has several layers of pure white petals that are easy to see in the dark. After one day, the white petals turn a dark, purplish pink. After another day, the petals die. Pea-sized seeds develop inside the flower.

giant lily pad and flower

Where They Live

A scientist named Thaddäus Haenke was the first European to report seeing a giant Amazon water lily. He saw it in Bolivia in 1803. It is said that he fell to his knees in astonishment at its size.

Today, giant water lilies are known to live not only in Bolivia, but also in Brazil, Argentina, and the Guiana region of South America. They grow on the waters of slow-moving rivers and lakes. Some grow in small rivers that dry up each year during the dry season, killing the plants. Others live in permanent bodies of water. In such places, the plants grow bigger every year.

Amazon water lilies can be grown in artificial pools, from seeds. They were first grown in artificial surroundings by Joseph Paxton in England in 1849.

Tropical plants were very popular in England at that time, and Paxton was well known for his success in getting tropical plants to grow.

We recognize two species of giant Amazon water lilies today, *Victoria amazonica* and *Victoria cruziana*. *Victoria amazonica* grows near the equator in South America, in hot climates. It must have water temperatures of 80 to 85° Fahrenheit (27 to 29°C). *Victoria cruziana* grows in cooler places, as far south as Argentina. Many of those that grow on display in Europe and North America are hybrids between the two species. These hybrids have the best qualities of both species. The Amazon lilies were given the name *Victoria* in honor of Queen Victoria, who reigned as queen of England from 1837 until her death in 1901. She said she was "immensely pleased" at the honor.

Amazon water lilies can be seen today at the Missouri Botanical Garden in St. Louis, at the New York Botanical Garden, and at Longwood Gardens in Pennsylvania. Longwood Gardens is the center for seed production. Many other gardens order seeds from them every year, because giant lilies displayed outdoors are killed by our cold North American winters. You can find out how to contact these botanical gardens in the "Resources" section of this book.

Lilies or Not?

Water lilies are not actually in the lily family (Liliaceae), which includes daylilies, lilies of the valley, Solomon's seals, wild onions, yucca plants, aloes, trilliums, and many more. All lily flowers have three petals, although the three leaves, or sepals, underneath the petals may look like more petals, making the flowers appear to have six petals.

Water lilies are in the family Nymphaeaceae. All members of this family are water plants and most are called water lilies. They are found all around the world in tropical and temperate climates. Many have round, floating leaves, which are often called lily pads. But some members of the family have leaves that grow underwater.

Water lilies that you may have seen growing wild in the United States probably belong to the genus *Nymphaea* or the genus *Nuphar*. *Nymphaea odorata* is a common water lily, found in lakes and ponds of the eastern United States. It has round, floating leaves that are about 8 to 12 inches wide. The leaves don't have the upturned rim of the Amazon water lily. The flowers have many white pointed petals and are 3 to 6 inches across.

The genus *Nuphar* has yellow flowers. One *Nuphar* species is commonly called cow lily or great yellow pond lily. It grows from Alaska through western Canada to California and Colorado, in ponds and slow-moving water. Its leaves may be 16 inches long and 10 inches wide. Its large flowers are deep yellow.

➤ Beetles of the Night ➤

Amazon water lilies are pollinated by large scarab beetles of the genus *Cyclocephala*, which fly about at night. The white color of the blossom is easily seen at night and is attractive to the beetles. The flower also produces a strong, sweet smell, sort of like pineapple, that appeals to the beetles. When the flower opens for the first time, at dusk, the beetles are drawn by the scent to the center of it. Here the flower has provided for their comfort. The flower heats the air in its center by breaking down starches in the flower cells. Night air is much cooler than daytime air, and insects need warmth in order to be active. While the beetles enjoy the warmth, they discover the flower's main attraction. The flower has a banquet laid out for them. Inside the center, the beetles find a circle of food knobs that contain sugars and starches. The beetles eat them greedily. The knobs are located directly over the top surface of the flower's female organ (the pistil). So if the beetles have pollen on their bodies, the pollen rubs off on the top of the pistil, called the stigma. The knobs have no other function than to feed the beetles and to lure them to the stigma. While the beetles are eating, the petals slowly close over them. The beetles are held pris-

oner for the rest of the night and through part of the next day. While they are inside, the flower's male parts (the anthers) mature and begin to release pollen. The beetles, still crawling around and feeding inside the flower, get pollen all over their bodies.

Later that day, the petals open again. The petals are no longer white, but have turned pink. All of the flowers that belong to a particular plant become pink at the same time. The beetles leave the flower, in search of a white flower, which will be on a different water lily plant. There they will find the food knobs, and as they eat, they will smear the pollen on their bodies onto the stigma of the new flower. The plant they've just come from will not produce new white flowers for another day yet.

In this way, the flowers of the giant Amazon water lily are pollinated. Once pollen is delivered, each egg in the ovary is fertilized by a single sperm cell and begins to develop into a seed. The flower sinks into the river and becomes a fruit. When the fruit and the seeds inside it are ripe, the fruit splits open. The seeds float to the surface. The current carries them away, to start new plants somewhere else.

Bladderworts

That's Strange!

The scientist was delighted that his favorite fish had finally laid some eggs in his aquarium. He'd been hoping for months that this would happen. Excitedly, he called a couple of his friends. Then he moved the parent fish out of the aquarium and removed an old water plant that looked ill. He wanted to make the aquarium as healthy and safe for the eggs as he could. They were a rare and valuable species. He hoped to sell them later to other science labs.

He knew that water plants can add oxygen to the water, and can provide hiding places for little fish. So he decided to get a fresh plant for the aquarium, from the pond near his office. He took his dip net down to the pond and chose a smallish plant that was mostly underwater. He scooped it up, put it in his pail, and then quickly took it up the hill to his aquarium. He settled the plant in the water, then returned to his studies, knowing that the eggs wouldn't hatch for several days.

Finally the day arrived when the tiny new fish began to break free of the eggs. Within a few hours, there were at least 40 little ones in the aquarium! Excitedly, he called one of his friends, another fish scientist, to tell her the good news. He invited the scientist to come over the next day to see the babies.

When his friend arrived the next morning, the two went into the lab to see the new arrivals. But they had a nasty surprise. Where were the little fish?! There were only three baby fish swimming around! Yet, there were no dead ones, either, none floating on top or lying on the bottom. "What is going on?" the baffled scientist barked to his friend.

Then, to his horror, he saw his tiny fish. Rather, he saw their heads and tails. Each missing fish had one end stuck in a tiny round trap. The underwater branches of the plant he'd brought in had dozens of tiny round traps on them, and the traps were *eating* his valuable fish!

bladderwort eating a small fish

How Do They Do That?

The underwater stems of bladderwort plants have hundreds of tiny sacs, or bladders, attached to them. Each bladder is able to suck in tiny prey. The bladder has a small opening at one end, with a little door that opens and closes. After the prey is sucked in, the door slams shut behind it.

How does the suction work? That's the trick. First of all, the trap has to be set. To be set, it has to be emptied. The bladder has glands in it that remove water from its inside. As it is emptied, the pressure inside the bladder becomes much lower than the pressure outside. The door at the opening of the bladder fits very tightly and keeps water from rushing in. The door is attached by its top edge to the bladder. It can swing open into the bladder, but it cannot swing out. Behind the door is a flap that presses against the door and helps seal the opening. The door gets more help from a collar of cells along the bottom of the opening. These cells produce a sticky goo that glues the door and the flap to the bottom of the opening, making a better seal.

If you could see a bladder up close, you would see two long and stiff trigger hairs sticking out from the door of the bladder. The trigger hairs are attached to the very edge of the door, right where it forms a tight seal against the bladder to keep water out. Can you guess what happens if something bumps up against a trigger hair? The stiff hair acts as a lever and pushes the edge of the door. Even the slightest push will break the seal. And because the pressure outside the bladder is greater than inside, the water rushes in, pushing the door up and out of the way. Whoever happens to be swimming outside the door gets swept inside as the water rushes in. Then the door whams shut and seals again. The glands inside the bladder begin removing the water again.

But whatever unfortunate creature is inside doesn't get pumped out. It stays for good. The bladder begins to secrete digestive enzymes that break

bladderwort

What They Look Like

There are over 200 species of bladderworts, all in the genus *Utricularia*. Most live in water, floating just below the surface. The stems are very thin and have threadlike branches. An entire bladderwort plant may be several feet long. Along the branches are the tiny oval-shaped bladders that trap small animals. The largest of bladders are $\frac{1}{5}$ inch (5 mm) long. But in most species the bladders are much smaller.

On floating bladderwort plants, the bladders are usually considered to be the leaves. But some **botanists** consider the stems to be the leaves. Other types of bladderworts that are rooted in the ground or that grow on moss may have obvious leaves that grow upright, to a length of several inches. Their bladders arise from some other part of the plant.

Bladderwort flowers are purple or yellow. The flowers of aquatic species are tiny and bloom above the surface on short stalks. The flowers of **terrestrial** (land dwelling) species may be larger.

down the creature's body. The nutrient broth is absorbed through the bladder walls and circulates through the rest of the plant.

How does a creature come to be right outside a bladder door? Tiny animals may be attracted by a faint odor. Once they are close to the bladder, they are guided toward the door by guard hairs that form a sort of funnel around the door. But the guard hairs play no part in breaking the seal and opening the door. Only the two trigger hairs do that.

When an animal longer than the bladder gets sucked in, the door reseals against the animal's body as water is moved out of the bladder. If the animal's thrashing hits a trigger hair again, then it gets sucked in a little further. Sooner or later, its whole body is pulled in.

Sometimes a fish or a wormlike insect larva will have its head sucked into one bladder and its tail end sucked into another bladder! In that case, neither bladder will get the whole thing. Each end will be digested while the middle part hangs in limbo. After a while, the middle will fall away to the pond floor.

A bladder is green when it is new or young. As it begins to fill up, it turns purplish. Sooner or later it will have too much undigested stuff inside. It will turn black and fall off the stem.

Where They Live

Bladderworts are found on every continent. Some species grow even in the Arctic and the Antarctic. Bladderwort species that have no roots live in small ponds or in the shallow edges of lakes, floating below the surface. Some of the species that have roots are found in very shallow water, with their roots in the ground under the water. Others with roots grow in soil that is very wet, but is not underwater. Still others live on top of wet moss that grows on trees or stones, in swampy areas. They don't eat the moss or take any nutrients from it. Rather, they grow as epiphytes. An epiphyte is a plant that grows on another plant, but takes its food from air, rainwater, and sunlight. Bladderworts are epiphytes that happen to also be meat-eaters, but not all epiphytes eat meat.

how the bladderwort's trap works

a. Long guard hairs funnel the prey toward the opening of the bladder.

b. The swimming prey touches the two trigger hairs attached to the edge of the door, breaking the seal.

c. The door swings inward and water rushes into the bladder, sweeping the prey in too.

d. The door slams shut and reseals, trapping the prey inside the bladder.

Acacia Trees

That's Strange!

If you looked at a bull's-horn acacia tree, it wouldn't necessarily seem like an odd plant. It's covered with thorns, but lots of plants have thorns. Roses do, blackberries and raspberries do. Thorns are no big deal.

Now, if you looked carefully at the acacia, you might notice that the thorns are pretty hefty, up to 2 inches long and very thick at the base. And you might notice bright orange beads at the tips of the leaflets. That's odd. Leaves with beads? What could the beads be for?

Still, all in all, it's just another short, shrubby, thorny tree. That is . . . until you touch it. Then it becomes a very odd tree indeed. Hordes of angry ants come running out of nowhere, ants with big stingers. And they deliver very unpleasant stings, to you or anyone else touching their tree. What kind of arrangement is this? Where did the ants come from? And what is their problem?

ants on an acacia tree

What They Look Like   Acacia trees are in the bean family. This is a large family that includes all of the familiar peas and beans that we eat. It also includes some familiar trees such as red-buds, mesquite, and all the types of locust trees.

Acacias and most other members of the bean family produce their seeds in a long pod. The pod is called a legume. Hence the family is called the legume family. When you eat ordinary table beans that we call green beans or string beans, you are eating bean pods with the seeds still inside the pods. When you eat baked beans or green peas, you're eating just the seeds, which have been removed from their pod. Peanuts are legumes. The peanut shell is the seed pod, the peanut is the seed.

In general, acacias are short, shrubby trees with lots of small leaflets and lots of thorns. The thorns discourage some animals that might otherwise eat the leaves and branches. But others, like giraffes, eat the branches, thorns and all.

The structure of an acacia leaf is a little unusual. Each leaf has a main stem, with several pairs of smaller stems branching off of it. Along each smaller stem are several pairs of small, oval leaflets.

The bull's-horn acacia is one of many acacia species that harbor ants. Those with ants have three features that other acacias don't. First, their thorns are large and swollen at the base. The thorns attach to the branches in pairs. Together, the two swollen thorns look like a bull's head with two horns. Second, acacias with ants have brightly colored beads on the tips of the leaflets. And third, ant acacias have swollen bumps at the base of each leaf stem.

acacia tree

Why Do They Do That?

Lumps, beads, and swollen thorns. Why? All of these features are to befriend the ants. How does a tree befriend an ant? The enlarged thorns that are found on some acacias are hollow inside, or may contain a soft, light plant material called pith. When a young ant queen, of a particular kind of ant, comes upon a new thorn on a young acacia tree, she chews a hole in the thorn and crawls in. She removes any pith inside the seed, and lays some eggs inside the thorn. When the eggs hatch, the queen feeds and cares for the young until they develop into worker ants. The thorn is their home. The queen lays more eggs in the thorn, and this time the new workers care for the young. As the ant colony grows, the ants may spread into other nearby thorns.

Some thorns may be occupied by other queens with their own colonies. Sooner or later, the workers of different colonies will fight until only one colony dominates the tree.

The tree has provided a home or a shelter for the ants by having swollen hollow thorns. The tree also provides food for the ants. The brightly colored beads on the tips of the leaflets are highly nutritious pellets of food. They are called Beltian bodies, after Thomas Belt, who described them in his 1874 book *The Naturalist in Nicaragua.* They are rich in oil and protein. The ants can easily pluck or snip the Beltian bodies from the leaflet tips and carry them around. The acacia provides the ants with a nutritious sweet drink, too —nectar. Nectar is really just sugary water, but it provides energy for the ants.

Nectar is very important in the plant world because it attracts pollen carriers. Ants are not very good for carrying pollen, though. They don't fly and they don't travel far enough. Yet the acacia makes nectar for the ants, anyway. This acacia nectar is not in a flower. It comes from the small lumps at the base of each leaf. It oozes out of a little hole in the lump, and the ants drink it up. We know this nectar is not there to attract pollinators because it's not in a flower. So why does the acacia provide all this stuff for the ant? Does the tree benefit from this relationship, too?

The ants do indeed help the tree. First of all, the workers take turns patrolling the tree 24 hours a day. Acacias are tropical trees and the tropics are teeming with plant-eating insects and other animals. If an insect lands on an acacia, the workers sting and kill it. If a mammal grabs or bites a branch, workers run out of the thorns to attack the creature. Insect eggs or larvae are killed and removed. This is a great service to the tree. The ants keep it from being eaten.

But that's not all. The ants also attack plants that might compete with their tree for space or water or light. Any plant that sprouts within about 6 inches of the tree's trunk is chewed up by the ants until it's dead. Any branch that touches the acacia's upper branches is boarded and chewed up.

Even after scientists learned about all the ways that ants help acacias, they still were not sure that the tree really needed the ants. Clearly the ants needed the tree, but wouldn't the tree be able to survive without the ants?

A scientist named Daniel Janzen answered this question with a famous experiment in the 1960s. Janzen wanted to compare the health of acacias with and without ants. To do this, he watched and measured two groups of new bull's-horn acacia shoots in Mexico for a year. He kept the ants off one group of shoots while he allowed the ants to stay on the other group of shoots. After a year, he weighed and measured shoots, counted leaves, and counted swollen thorns. The shoots that had ants protecting them were far bigger, healthier, and more numerous. They also had far more leaves and swollen thorns. Many of the shoots without ant protection died. Why? The acacias with no ants to protect them were seriously damaged by plant-eating insects. So Janzen proved that the acacia trees most definitely benefit from their relationship with the ants.

A relationship like this between two species of living things, is called **mutualism.** In a mutualistic relationship, both species provide a service to the other and both benefit from the relationship. There are many examples of mutualistic relationships in nature, but this is probably the best understood one between an ant species and a plant. Other examples of mutualistic relationships are the leaf-cutter ants and the fungus that they culture, birds that are known to eat parasitic insects from the skin of large mammals (such as the oxpecker bird and the hoofed animals of the African plains), fish that clean the teeth of hippopotamuses, fish that remove and eat parasites from larger fish, and so on.

The acacia ants and the acacia trees did not simply stumble upon one another, with all these helpful behaviors and structures already in place. Rather, the ants and the acacias changed together gradually over time. When ants first began to wander onto acacias, the acacias did not have all the structures that serve ants today. But some small change occurred randomly in an acacia, a change that happened to favor ants. Ants began to be attracted to the plant. Because the ants killed other insects, as many types of ants do, then other plant changes that favored ants were passed on in the plant population. Individual plants that had the genes for the change survived better, and so were able to pass the genes on to future plant generations.

This slow process of two species changing over time in response to each other is called **coevolution.** The changes happen for the selfish interests of each party. That is, the acacia didn't change just to be nice to the ants. The changes in the plant happened because the developing relationship helped the plant to survive. Likewise, the ants take part in this relationship because it helps the ants to survive.

Where They Live

Acacia trees live in the dry tropics of Latin America and Africa. A few species of acacia are found in the southwestern United States, but they are not species that attract and support ants. Many species of acacia don't have ant populations. Some acacias on islands and in high mountains where there are no acacia ants have evolved chemical defenses instead. Their leaves have developed chemicals that keep plant-eaters away.

Giant Kelp Forests

That's Strange!

In some ways this forest is like others you've visited. The "trees" stand tall, as tall as 100 feet (30 m). Their tops are bathed in sunlight, while the forest floor is dark. Scattered shafts of light filter through here and there. The trees in this forest make food for the resident animals. But the animals here are not the ones you're accustomed to seeing in a forest. There are no squirrels, no deer, no mice, no songbirds. The giant kelp forest is under-water. To visit it, you would need oxygen tanks and other scuba gear. In this beautiful forest, you might see a blue shark or a gray whale cruise by. You would see bright red kelp crabs, green kelp bass, turban snails, and orange sea slugs. You would also see brightly colored sea stars, lots of brittle stars, purple sea urchins, and red sea urchins. If you were very lucky, you might see the star of the show, a sea otter. In many kelp forests, the sea otter holds it all together.

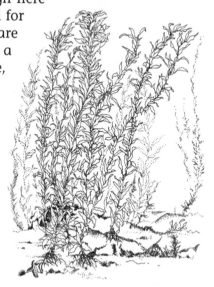

kelp forest

What They Look Like Giant kelp is a type of algae (singular *alga;* plural *algae*). Scientists no longer consider algae to be in the plant kingdom. They are instead in the kingdom Protista. Algae are much simpler than most plants. They do not have leaves, stems, roots, or complex reproductive structures such as flowers or cones. Some kinds of algae consist of only a single microscopic cell. Still, algae have some characteristics of plants and are often casually referred to as plants. Those species that live in the ocean are often called seaweed. The term "seaweed" also includes certain kinds of flowering grasses that live in the ocean.

Three major groups of algae are the green algae, red algae, and brown algae. Giant kelp is a type of brown algae. Almost all species of brown algae live in the ocean, along coasts. They grow on rocks in water up to about 100 feet (30 m) deep. Although they contain the same green pigment **chloro-phyll** that makes land plants look green, the brown algae look brown, olive green, or black. They have another pigment that covers up the chlorophyll. If you live near a coast you may have seen a type of common brown algae called rockweed or bladder wrack. It grows in slippery masses on rocks that are uncovered at low tide. Each plant is 1 to 3 feet (30 to 91 cm) long.

The largest of the brown algae are the kelps. More than 20 kelp species are found along the west coast of North America. The very largest are the giant kelps *(Macrocystis pyrifera)*. They are limited in height by the depth of the water, but that doesn't stop them from growing. The tops simply flop over and spread out over the surface of the water. These kelps often wind up over 100 feet long. Because they are so much larger than other kinds of seaweeds, they are sometimes called "the sequoias of the sea." Giant kelps grow close together and may extend for many miles of coastal water, creating a sort of forest.

Each plant is attached at one end to a rock or rocks on the ocean floor. It is anchored to the rocks by a spread-out tangle of rootlike structures called a **holdfast.** The holdfast has lots of small protected spaces where tiny animals can live. Unlike plant roots, the holdfast does not absorb nutrients. Its job is just to hold on.

Long, flexible stalks called **stipes** grow straight up out of the holdfast. These form the "trunk" or "trunks" of the "tree." The straplike "leaves" of a giant kelp are called **blades.** They are long, narrow, flat, and floppy. Blades are not true leaves, but, like leaves, their job is to catch sunlight. At the base of each blade, between the blade and its stipe, is a round bladder or bulb filled with air. These bulbs work like floats or fishing corks, causing the whole plant to stretch toward the surface.

A long stipe with its blades is sometimes called a frond. The fronds are flexible, swaying and bending gracefully with the rhythm of the waves and underwater currents. They are thick and lush, blocking out much of the sunlight. But when the sun is overhead, scattered rays break through. Scuba divers love to swim through giant kelp forests. They say that the beams of sunlight dancing through the swaying fronds are a beautiful sight. They enjoy seeing the great variety of creatures that live in a kelp forest, too.

On the surface of the water over a kelp forest, the floating tops of the plants form a lumpy mat. Sea otters rest in these mats. Their dark bodies are hard to spot, blending in with the dark lumps of kelp.

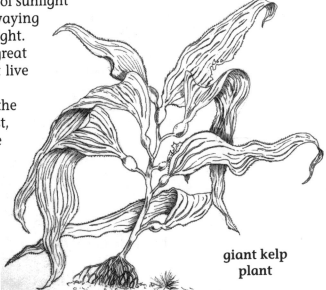

giant kelp plant

Why Do They Do That?

Like tropical rain forests and coral reefs, giant kelp forests provide homes for hundreds of different kinds of animals. These underwater forests are among the most diverse communities on earth. (A community is a group of living things in a given area that depend on one another for survival.) The holdfast alone, clinging to the rocks below, has nooks and crannies galore. One scientist estimated that a single large holdfast can provide homes for more than 100,000 animals large enough to see with the naked eye. If microscopic animals are included, then the total is much more. Many of them are small crustaceans, worms, and mollusks such as clams and sea slugs. Skinny little brittle stars anchor themselves inside their holdfast hideouts, reaching out to snag tiny bits of food floating by. Sea stars creep over the holdfast looking for prey. Hermit crabs search the edge of the holdfast for dead animals and bits of kelp.

On the stipes, or trunks, of the kelp plant are large turban snails and smaller top snails. The snails feed on dead parts of the stipe. Small and slender clingfish attach themselves to the kelp with a suction cup on their underside, hiding from larger fish. Spider crabs and bright red kelp crabs move up and down the stipes. On the blades that form the canopy of the kelp forest live bryozoans and hydrozoans—tiny animals that form a sort of frosting over the surface of the blades. Hundreds of creatures drift, creep, or swim through the spaces between plants, feeding on each other and on bits of kelp. Kelp bass, rockfish, giant kelpfish, and dozens of other fish seek shelter and food among the kelp fronds. Jellyfish and comb jellies float through. Those that get hung up in the kelp become food for bright orange-red sea stars.

Crustaceans, worms, mollusks, sea urchins, and fish live in the rocks below the kelp, feeding on broken and fallen pieces of kelp. These **scavengers** become prey to many predators that lurk in the rocks—octopuses, squids, sea anemones, colorful sea slugs, and bigger fish. Seals and sharks come through chasing fish, and even whales pass through occasionally.

The most popular of the kelp creatures is the sea otter. At zoos and aquaria where they are displayed in captivity, crowds gather to watch and admire them. They are sleek and graceful in water, with beautiful silver fur. The furry round face with black eyes and a black nose has the same appeal as a kitten or a bear cub.

Some kinds of otters spend time on land and in water, but sea otters live almost their entire lives in the ocean. Otters are **mammals**, so they breathe air. They are **warm-blooded** and have very thick fur to protect them from cold ocean water. They clean their fur frequently and blow air into it. The air forms a dry, warm layer next to their skin.

Sea otters are well adapted to life in the ocean. Giant kelp plays a big part in their lives. The otters often rest and sleep while floating on their backs among the kelp fronds. They may drape a blade of kelp over themselves to keep from drifting away. When mother otters have babies, they often park the babies in the kelp at the surface while they dive under the surface to find food.

sea otter
floating in
kelp

And what do sea otters eat? They eat shellfish and sea urchins, among other things. Many of the shellfish they eat are closed up tightly in protective shells. An otter can use its hands to pry a limpet (a snail with a cone-shaped shell) or other animal off of a rock below. The otter lies on its back on the water's surface to eat the shellfish. It may open the shell with its teeth. But if the shell is too hard and thick the otter will use a tool. It will bring up a rock from below, put the rock on its chest, and whack the shellfish repeatedly against the rock until the shell cracks. Then the animal inside is eaten.

Scientist James Estes and others have studied the sea urchins and kelp on the coasts of the Aleutian Islands near Alaska. They have found that the northern sea otters there are very important to the health of their kelp forests. This is because the otters eat so many sea urchins. These scientists have discovered that when sea otters are not present, sea urchins sometimes increase in numbers. Then the urchins may use up their other seaweed foods and begin to attack the giant kelp plants where they attach to the rocks. Their gnawing breaks the kelp loose and it is carried away on ocean currents. The urchins can wind up detaching all of the kelp in the area when sea otters are not present to keep their numbers in check. Such a kelpless place is called a "sea urchin barrens." All of the animals that depend on the kelp for food or shelter also perish.

What would cause sea otters to disappear? Humans in the past nearly wiped out sea otters entirely, hunting them for their dense and soft fur. But with legislation to protect them, they began to make a comeback. Yet, they are still very vulnerable to oil spills and water pollution. And just within the last few years, killer whales in certain areas have begun eating sea otters in great numbers, particularly in the Aleutian Islands off of Alaska's west coast. This has never been a problem before—killer whales in this area have usually eaten seals and sea lions. It is thought that the killer whales have begun to eat sea otters because seal and especially sea lion populations have decreased in number. Many scientists believe that overfishing by humans in the Bering Sea between Alaska and Asia has left too few fish for the sea lions. Some people think that changes in ocean temperatures may have changed fish populations, too. But whatever the reason, killer whales are now eating sea otters. In the west-central chain of the Aleutian Islands, sea otters once numbered 53,000. But they have dropped to just 6,000 in the last 8 to 10 years. These northern sea otters seem to be facing extinction unless something is done. The kelp forests in this area are dependent upon sea otters to control sea urchin populations. So the kelp forests are suffering, too, as well as all of the animals that live in and on the kelp.

This unhappy story is an example of the interconnectedness of all living things. We all affect each other on this planet, in ways that we often can't foresee. No one predicted that overfishing the Bering Sea would starve sea lions, which would starve killer whales and cause them to eat sea otters, which would then allow sea urchin populations to overgrow and kill kelp forests in the islands' coastal waters, thereby killing millions of other animals. What's the solution? Since we humans have a lot more choices about what to eat than animals do, perhaps we should back off on our consumption of certain oceanic fish. If you would like to ask for stricter fishing limits in the Bering Sea, you can write to the National Marine Fisheries Service, whose address is given below. Ask them to reduce the damage from commercial fishing, and ask them to do what is necessary to support the health of the entire ecosystem—the sea lions, otters, killer whales, and kelp forests.

Send your letter about reducing damage from commercial fisheries in the Bering Sea to:

Rolland Schmitten, Assistant Administrator for Fisheries
National Marine Fisheries Service
1315 E-W Highway
Silver Spring, MD 20910-3282

Where They Live

Kelp forests are found around the world. They grow on the west coast of North America from Alaska to Baja California, on the west coast and southeast coast of South America, along the southern tip of Africa, the southern tip of Australia, and the Pacific islands off the coast of southeast Australia.

Sea otters are found in California, but not Washington or Oregon. In these three western states, other animals help to keep the sea urchins under control so that kelp fronds can survive without otters.

You can see giant kelp in the huge Kelp Forest exhibit at the Monterey Bay Aquarium in Monterey, California. It grows in a tank that is 28 feet tall and 66 feet long. The tank has clear acrylic panels along one side that allow visitors to see the giant kelp from an underwater perspective, along with other seaweeds and many of the fish and invertebrate species associated with kelp.

For more information about giant kelp, you can contact the aquarium:

Monterey Bay Aquarium
886 Cannery Row
Monterey, CA 93940
Phone: 831 648-4888
www.montereybayaquarium.org

Rafflesias

That's Strange!

It spent 9 months as a big brown swelling. Now it's open and it's meat-red. Three feet wide, and a hefty 36 pounds. And it stinks. It smells like a dead animal. Flies that love stinky stuff flock to it. Maybe it *is* a dead animal. What else besides a carcass would be that red, that big, and smell that bad? Could it be a dead dog in the road? A pig? A young deer? No, it's a flower! The biggest flower anywhere in the world!

What They Look Like

A rafflesia flower makes its first appearance as a dark lump that looks a bit like a brown cabbage on the forest floor. This lump is the flower bud. The size of the resulting flower varies, depending upon which species of rafflesia it is. The smallest of the 13 species has a flower about the size of a saucer or a plate. The largest rafflesia flower is the 3-foot red blossom of *Rafflesia arnoldii*.

All of the rafflesias have the same basic flower structure—a bowl-shaped center surrounded by five thick, fleshy petals. All are red or orange with a pattern of white or cream-colored spots. The spots are raised like welts or huge mosquito bites. If you looked down inside the central bowl of the flower, you would see a round disk on a thick stalk. The top of the disk is covered with tall spikes. The male and female parts of the flower are under the edge of the disk, at the top of the curving stalk that supports it.

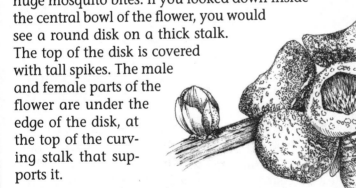

rafflesia flower

Why Do They Do That?

No one is really sure why rafflesias are so big. Some people guess that the large size helps the flower make more of the stinky odor.

Why does it have the stinky odor? Why would a flower smell like a carcass? A sweet-smelling flower may attract bees and butterflies, but some insects are drawn to foul smells. Many species of flies are attracted to the smell of dead animals because they lay their eggs on **carrion**, or rotting flesh. Have you ever seen a decomposing animal or piece of meat that had maggots on it? The maggots hatched from fly eggs that were laid on the carcass. The maggots, or fly larvae, live on the rotting meat and eat it until they have grown as large as they can. Then they go through a changing stage, called a **pupa**. After that stage, they are adult flies.

Flies that are attracted to a rotting carcass will also be attracted to a rafflesia and other kinds of flowers that have a carrion odor. Hey, if it *smells* like meat, it must *be* meat. Their little fly brains are programmed to respond to the smell. Many **carrion flies** will go so far as to lay their eggs inside flowers that smell like carrion. When their young hatch from the eggs as tiny maggots, there's nothing to eat, of course. All they *can* eat is rotten meat. So the maggots quickly starve to death. But the mother fly is already on her merry way, never to know her mistake. The flower has tricked the mother fly. The carrion smell is like a billboard that says "Right this way! Free dinner for all the kids!" But it's false advertising. There is no dinner at all. The flies are cheated. But the plant gets just what it needs—a pollen delivery service. Not a very fair trade.

Why would a rafflesia flower need to attract carrion flies? While mommy fly is looking for the source of the bad smell inside the flower so she can lay her eggs, she crawls over the edge of the central disk, onto the underside. This is where the rafflesia flower's sex organs are located, the organs that give and receive pollen. As she crawls around under the rim, she may bump up against a male part of the flower, a stamen, and get a gob of gooey pollen stuck on her back. Then later, in another rafflesia flower, she may rub her back against a female flower part, a pistil, and deliver the pollen. This is all accidental on the part of the fly. But it's important because pollen contains the sperm cells necessary for fertilizing an egg in the female organ of a flower. Once an egg is fertilized, it can grow into a seed. The pistil that contains the seed or seeds develops into a fruit.

After fertilization occurs in a *Rafflesia arnoldii* flower, a big, brown fruit develops. It's about the size of a coconut, with a woody surface like a coconut. There are thousands of seeds in its oily greenish white flesh. Many plants other than rafflesias produce seeds inside fleshy fruits. Tasty fruit attracts animals that spread seeds around to new places, which is a good thing for the plants.

The rafflesia flower was first discovered by European explorers in 1818, on an expedition into Sumatra led by Sir Thomas Stamford Raffles. For 173 years after that, no one knew what kinds of animals ate the fruit. Some suggested elephants, others thought insects. In 1991, two scientists named Louise Emmons and Jamili Nais hid in a tree for several hours to discover that squirrels and shrews eat the fruit of rafflesia. They guess that the seeds get caught in the rodents' teeth and claws and get spread around to new locations when the animals grab and chew on other things.

Where They Live

Rafflesia species grow in the rain forests of tropical Asia—in Thailand, Malaysia, Indonesia, and the Philippines. The largest, *Rafflesia arnoldii*, is found in Sumatra, which is part of Indonesia.

A Challenger to the Champ

Rafflesia arnoldii is the world's largest flower. But another plant, the titan arum, can claim the title of "world's largest inflorescence." The giant bloom is 3 feet (1 m) wide and 9 feet (3 m) tall! That's a lot bigger than a rafflesia. So why is rafflesia considered to be the biggest flower? The titan arum looks like a single flower, but it isn't. It's really a cluster of tiny flowers. A cluster of flowers that may appear to be a single flower is called an **inflorescence**. This gigantic arum is related to skunk cabbage and jack-in-the-pulpit, discussed in the first chapter. Like its relatives, the titan arum has a tall spadix in the center of the bloom. Small flowers without petals are imbedded in the spadix. The 9-foot-tall spadix of the titan arum sits inside a 4-foot-tall, cup-shaped spathe, like a tall candle in a teacup.

The titan arum grows on the ground in the rain forests of central Sumatra in Indonesia. It begins life as a seed, which first develops into a single leaf. The one leaf may stand up to 20 feet (6 m) tall, as tall as a two-story building! The leaf dies each year and is replaced by a new one. Each leaf, in its turn, makes food from photosynthesis and stores it underground in a huge swollen root called a corm. After several years, the leaf is not replaced when it dies. Instead, the big corm produces the huge titan arum inflorescence with its giant spadix. Like *Rafflesias* and like some of the other arums, the titan arum bloom has the smell of rotten meat. The stench attracts flies, which carry the titan's pollen around, to fertilize the female flowers on other titan arums.

Fertilized female flowers on the lower part of the spadix develop into huge red berries all around the lower spadix. Each berry is several inches long. The rest of the inflorescence dies and falls away. The stem at the base of the spadix grows taller, pushing the spadix and the pretty red berries 6 or 7 feet (2 m) into the air, where birds can find them. Birds called hornbills eat the berries and carry the seeds away to grow in a new place. The plant feeds the hornbills and the hornbills help to establish a new generation of plants. Once again, we see how living things depend upon one another. If one disappears from the planet, will the others be able to survive? Unfortunately, the answer is often "no."

titan arum inflorescence

The Biggest Flower in the World is a Parasite!

All rafflesias are parasites. A parasite lives and feeds on another living thing, without killing it (at least not right away). Rafflesias are parasites of tropical vines in the genus *Tetrastigma*. These vines are in the same plant family as grapevines.

Rafflesias have no leaves, no branches, no roots! They don't need these things because the vine that they parasitize provides all of their food and water for them. The rafflesia plant consists only of the parts that allow it to reproduce—the bud, the flower, and the fruit, plus the tiny threads that invade the vine and rob it of **nutrients.**

The life of a rafflesia begins when an animal wipes a tiny rafflesia seed onto a *Tetrastigma* vine, close to the ground. The seed sprouts and small, threadlike growths called haustoria creep into the vine. The threads form a band, like an armband, around the sap vessels inside the vine. If you were to look at the vine at this time, you would see a ring of swelling under the bark. The threads, or haustoria, then merge into the vessels of the vine, so that the parasite can draw nutrients from the vine. After awhile a lump develops on the vine's bark. It gets bigger and bigger and develops into a huge flower bud. When the bud finally opens, voilà—the world's largest flower!

Underground Orchids

That's Strange!

One fine winter day in 1928, Mr. John Trott was working on his farm in western Australia. He had burned some brush to clear a section of his land, and now he was plowing the burned area. His plow broke through some old underground stumps. He hopped off of his tractor to have a look, and he saw something odd. He saw some whitish stems that looked something like white stalks of asparagus. They had been underground until the plow turned the soil and uncovered them. We don't know what he thought at that first glimpse, but he may have wondered if they were some kind of fungus. Mushrooms and their underground networks are often whitish. Or maybe he thought they were just some old dead sticks, whitened from age and the loss of their bark. Maybe he guessed they were roots, which are often whitish. But then he looked at the white stalks carefully and decided that they were none of those things. He ruled out fungi, sticks, and roots because each of the stalks had a single, fleshy, whitish flower at one end of it! The stalks were alive and well, the flowers were alive and well, and all of them had been completely buried for some time! Imagine his amazement. These stalks were living plants that were entirely underground and were even blooming underground! He had discovered the world's first underground orchid.

What They Look Like

The orchid that Mr. Trott discovered was named *Rhizanthella gardneri*. *Rhiz* means "rootlike," and *anthella* means "little flower." Mr. Trott turned over the odd little stalks and flowers to a scientist named C. A. Gardner, who realized with great excitement that they were orchids, and shared this discovery with the scientific world. Our knowledge of the flowers is based largely on Dr. Gardner's description of them, and so the species was named after him.

Each stalk of *Rhizanthella* appears to bear a single flower, but that flower is really a cluster of tiny red and purple flowers inside a ring of pink, fleshy, petal-like structures. The arrangement of the tiny flowers and the "petals" is something like the arrangement on the head of a daisy. A daisy is also a cluster of tiny flowers surrounded by a ring of petals. If you look very closely at a daisy in bloom, you can see all the tiny flowers in the center.

**underground orchid,
*Rhizanthella***

The stalk of *Rhizanthella* is white and only a few inches long. Its leaves, over evolutionary time, have become smaller and smaller until now they are only whitish scales that lie flat on the stalk. There are no leaves other than the scales.

The lower end of the stalk is attached to a thick underground stem. This stem, called a rhizome, may be a foot deep. Like the flower stalk, it has scales on it. The rhizome may have short, branchlike buds that will develop into new sections of rhizome. The old rhizome dies after the flowers have bloomed.

The rhizome also has fine white hairs on it, whose job is to collect water and nourishment. There are no true roots, so the rhizome and its hairs have to perform the roots' job.

underground orchid,
Rhizanthella

How Do They Do That?

Rhizanthella is very rare, or at least very rarely seen. Until 1979, it had been spotted in nature only seven times. It is so rare that scientists don't want to remove it from nature, because that usually means killing it. So they study it where it is. At present there are several *Rhizanthella* sites that have been roped off for scientific work. The plants are protected and studied without digging them up.

These underground orchids not only look very odd, but their way of life is very odd, too. They have no leaves, and they have no roots. They are missing two very important organs that almost all flowering plants have. Imagine you discovered a type of jungle cat that had no stomach and no feet! That's how odd *Rhizanthella* is.

Most plants need leaves in order to make food. The green pigment in a leaf, called chlorophyll, absorbs sunlight. The chlorophyll in a leaf pulls the energy out of the sunlight and traps it chemically, in sugar molecules. The sugar is stored in the leaf, in the form of starch. Then the plant uses that stored energy to run the machinery of life. That energy fuels its growth, and allows it to heal from injuries.

A plant that has chlorophyll in it will be green, unless the green is covered up by a darker color. *Rhizanthella* has no chlorophyll, not even in the stalk or the rhizome. Even if it did, there is no sunlight underground. So chlorophyll would not be useful. Well, then, how can the little orchid live and grow? *Rhizanthella* must get its energy in some other way.

If you have already read the chapters on rafflesias and mistletoes, then you may have guessed that the underground orchid is a parasite. If you did, you're right. But *Rhizanthella* is a different kind of parasite. While mistletoe and the giant flower Rafflesia steal their nutrients from other plants, the underground orchid takes its nutrients from a *fungus!* And the fungus is at the same time taking nutrients from nearby trees and shrubs! Here's how the three-way partnership works. Tiny threads of the fungus grow all around the little hairs on the underground orchid stem. They enter the hairs and then the stem itself. The fungal threads go inside some of the storage cells in the orchid stem. Inside a cell, the thread forms a coil. Meanwhile, other threads that are part of the same body of fungus are growing next to the roots of shrubs and eucalyptus trees in the area. The fungal threads don't invade these tree and shrub roots, but they do steal certain nutrients from them. The stolen nutrients travel throughout the netlike body of the underground fungus and into the fungal threads that are inside the cells of the underground orchid stem. The orchid cells then digest the nutrient-rich fungal threads.

Rhizanthella cannot live and grow without this particular type of fungus, which is called *Rhizoctonia.* The trees or shrubs must be present, too, to provide the nutrients. You can see why it is very hard or impossible to grow *Rhizanthella* in a pot or garden. You'd have to transplant trees, shrubs, and big areas of soil and fungus along with the little orchid.

This arrangement between *Rhizanthella* and the fungus sounds peculiar, but it exists for a shorter period in many other orchids. Many species of orchids are dependent on fungi to get their seeds going. Fungal threads must invade the cells of the embryo, or the tiny plant inside the seed. The threads coil inside the cells, just as they do in the underground stem of *Rhizanthella.* The fungal threads carry nutrients into the cells and grow plump, then the cells digest the coils. After the seed sprouts and grows leaves, the embryo no longer needs the fungus, because the new leaves can make the food it needs.

In a sense, *Rhizanthella* has just continued the embryo's arrangement into adulthood.

Who Will Bring Me My Pollen?

Most flowering plants in the world rely on wind or animals to carry pollen from male flowers to female flowers. Those animals are usually bees, butterflies, hummingbirds, or other small flying animals. But what can help an underground flower? When *Rhizanthella* flowers are mature, the male and female parts are just below the surface. The opening of the thick "petals" often cracks the ground just a little bit above the flowers. Scientists believe that small flies enter the cracks in the ground and visit the flowers, carrying pollen from male flower parts to female flower parts. They believe that underground termites may also carry pollen from one flower to another!

Another Underground Orchid

Rhizanthella gardneri is not the only underground orchid. There is one more, called *Cryptanthemis slateri*. It was discovered 3 years after the discovery of *Rhizanthella,* also in Australia. It is very similar to *Rhizanthella,* lacking leaves and roots. It differs, though, in having three or four branches off each vertical stalk. Each branch has its own flowering head. *Rhizanthella* has only one flowering head per stalk. *Cryptanthemis* is even more rare than its underground relative. It has been found only three times!

Indian Pipe

There is a common woodland wildflower that shares some of *Rhizanthella*'s oddest traits. If you walk in the woods frequently, you may have seen it. It is called Indian pipe, because the single droopy flower and its stalk look like the bowl and stem of a pipe. The whole plant is entirely white! The stalk rises above the ground about 4 to 6 inches (10 to 15 cm). The flower is about ¾ inch (2 cm) long. The small, thin, white leaves lie flat against the stalk, useless. Like the underground orchids, Indian pipe draws all of its nutrients from underground fungi. You can tell it has no chlorophyll because it's white instead of green. And without chlorophyll, it is unable to make its own sugars by photosynthesis. The fungus that feeds Indian pipe gets food from nearby green plants. So, it's another three-way arrangement. The fungus and the plant that provide the food are both essential to the survival of the Indian pipe.

Neither the Indian pipe nor the underground orchids give anything back to the fungus, or to the green plant that provides food to the fungus. So like the orchids, Indian pipe is a parasite.

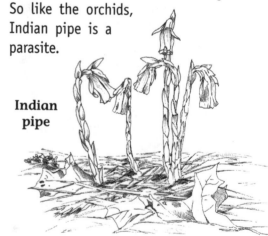

Indian
pipe

Where They Live

The underground orchids are found only in Australia and are very, very rare. Indian pipe is widespread throughout North America, from Alaska to Mexico. Because it needs no sunlight, it can grow in deep shade where it has little competition from short green plants dependent on the Sun. It is most common in pine woodlands, where the ground is clear of other short growth. But it can also be found in **deciduous** woodlands, where trees have broad leaves rather than needles.

Strangler Figs

That's Strange!

The anaconda grabbed the young pig with its teeth and then quickly wrapped its body around the struggling, squealing animal. The pig was soon covered by tight and heavy snake coils. Luisa and Miguel were horrified. Their mother would be furious. She had told them to keep a close watch on the pig. But they had been playing and had forgotten all about it. Now what could be done? The children kicked at the snake, then pulled on its coils. Not even a flinch of response. Luisa picked up a thick stick and whacked at the snake. Even as she beat at it, she could see the coils tightening. The pig was unable to breathe and would be dead soon if it wasn't already. Poor pig! Miguel began to cry. "Cruel snake! Let go of our pig!" Luisa screamed in anger. The children ran back to the village to get help, leaving the snake and the pig to complete their drama in private.

On the other side of the village, another drama unfolded. Another victim was slowly being squeezed to death. But this time no one noticed. Because the victim did not squeal or struggle. And the murder took years to complete. The killer was a strangler fig, and the victim a palm tree. Like the anaconda, the strangler fig wrapped itself around and around its victim. It slowly squeezed the palm until the vessels under its bark could no longer move nutrients up and down the trunk. So hard that the palm choked and died. No amount of beating or kicking could induce the fig to let go or unwrap itself, not that anyone tried. Long after Luisa and Miguel had grown up, the dead palm slowly fell apart, leaving the strangler fig standing in its place.

strangler fig and tree victim

What They Look Like A strangler fig is easy to recognize. In the early stages of its life, it may look like a couple of smooth gray vines wrapped tightly around another tree. These vines are really roots. The roots grow to be broad and flattened, and look molded to the tree like octopus tentacles. They're not just dangling there; they fit very snugly around the other tree. On an older strangler fig, the roots have branched and spread, have grown over one another, and have partly grown together. These fused and overlapping roots form a strong and sturdy trunk. If the strangler fig has been standing for a long time, the tree that it has wrapped itself around will be dead and gone. In this case, the inside of the strangler's trunk will be empty.

Strangler figs can grow as tall as 60 feet, and have an umbrella-like crown that provides shade over a large area. Although the trunk is unusual, the branches and leaves of a strangler are not remarkable. Each leaf is 4 to 6 inches (10 to 15 cm) long and oval in shape, with a point at the tip. The fruits, called figs, are much like those of the other 900 or so species of fig trees. They are soft, tasty, and full of small seeds. The figs attract dozens of species of mammals and birds.

When a section of rain forest is cut by a timber company, or by local people wanting farmland, the strangler figs are often the only ones left standing. Their wood is no good for lumber, and the shade is valuable in the hot tropics.

How Do They Do That?

How does one tree strangle another one? It can't slither over and grab its victim, as an anaconda does. Animals move with muscles, and plants have no muscles. But plants can move by growth. This is how the strangler fig attacks its victim.

Growth from where to where? You might guess that a strangler fig begins life as a seed that sprouts on the ground, then grows up toward the sky. This is how trees normally begin life. But the strangler fig has a backward kind of early life. It does grow from a seed, but the seed doesn't sprout on the ground. It sprouts in the sky and then grows down until it touches the ground! This backward way of doing things sets it up perfectly for its murderous habits.

To understand how and why the seed of a strangler fig begins life in the sky, we've got to go back for a minute to the fruit—the fig that this seed came from. Many types of trees make tasty fruits so that animals will eat the fruits and carry the seeds away in their bodies. The seeds pass through the animals' bodies unharmed, and are dropped in some fresh new place where the seeds have space to grow, away from the shade and roots of their parents. This is an important way that trees are able to spread their offspring around to a variety of new places. If none of their seeds were ever carried away, the seeds would all try to grow near the parent tree and all of the plants would become very crowded.

The seeds of figs get spread around in this way, too. Monkeys, bats, parrots, macaws, and other animals of the rain forest treetops eat lots of figs. As they move away through the forest, they leave their droppings here and there on other trees. The seeds of a strangler fig have a sticky covering. If a bird or mammal leaves a pile of droppings in the top of a tall tree, then a fig seed in the pile may sprout there. If it does, it will first send down a little root. The little root that comes from a fig seed is called an aerial root, because it spends a long time traveling downward through the air. (Your average root travels through soil.) The aerial root grows down and down from the treetop, toward the ground. If it passes a hole or a cranny where dead plant matter has piled up a little, it will send out some little rootlets to take nutrients from the dead stuff. (You can read more about aerial roots in the chapter on mangroves.)

The root continues on its way until it finally reaches the ground. It then moves down into the soil as any root would and begins pulling nutrients from the soil. The nutrients travel up the aerial root to the seed in the treetop. Then the seed sends a shoot upward in search of sunlight.

Leaves form and grow on the shoot. The shoot branches and more leaves grow. The aerial root branches, too, and grows downward. As the roots grow they begin to take on the woody texture of a tree trunk. They grow wide and flat. Many of the new roots grow in a spiral around the trunk of the host tree, until they reach the ground. (In nature, a host is a plant or animal that another plant or animal lives on.)

Over time the leaves and shoots grow taller than the host tree and begin to keep sunlight from reaching the host's leaves. This weakens the host tree, which needs sunlight to carry out photosynthesis.

At the same time, the growing and spreading roots are covering more and more of the trunk. The roots are very hard, just like the big branches of a tree. As the roots overlap each other and fuse together, they form a tight cylinder around the trunk of the host tree. They keep the trunk of the host tree from growing and expanding over time. This is what really strangles the tree. After awhile, the trunk of the host can no longer carry nutrients back and forth from leaves to roots. At the same time, the strangler fig's underground roots are sucking up water and nutrients that the host needs, too. The host tree slowly dies. It decays, and slowly falls apart. Bacteria, fungi, beetles, termites, and other organisms play their part in breaking down the dead tree. After a long time the dead host is gone. It has returned to the soil. Only the strangler remains. A strange tree with a hollow center and a trunk of gnarled and tangled, flattened and spiraling roots.

At Home with a Strangler

The trunk of a mature strangler fig is made up of a great many aerial roots and rootlets that lie across one another at odd angles. This crisscrossing creates a trunk with a great variety of spaces. There are holes, caves, cracks, pockets, slits, and caverns everywhere on the surface of the tree. Nearly all of these spaces become home to something or someone. Some animals come and go, others spend their entire lives on the trunk of a single strangler fig.

Social insects build colonies in and on the strangler. Many species of wasps build nests in the dry, protected cavities on a strangler fig trunk. There may be thousands of wasps in a single colony. These wasps can deliver painful stings to protect themselves from monkeys or birds that might try to steal the wasp larvae for food.

Stingless bees may make their nests in the soft, rotting wood of the host tree. Some colonies gnaw a narrow passageway to their nest, through the much harder wood of the fig tree. This narrow opening to the outside world is easy to guard, which helps them stay safe from army ants and other raiders.

Carpenter ants also build nests in the soft wood of the dying host tree. Many ants of other species come and go, looking for food and then moving on.

Colorful male lizards stake out territories on the tree trunks, keeping other males of the same species away. Females are welcomed and are **courted** by the males, who are eager for mates.

Bats, birds, and monkeys perch in the branches of strangler figs, gorging themselves on the sweet figs. Some bat species eat almost nothing but figs. As the monkeys scamper through the limbs, many figs are knocked to the ground, where they are eaten by insects, peccaries, agoutis, and other animals. Peccaries are small wild pigs and agoutis are cat-sized rodents. Many of these animals are dependent on the strangler fig for their home and livelihood.

Where They Live

Strangler figs grow in the tropics and subtropics of North and South America. In the United States, they grow only in the southern tip of Florida.

━━◀ A Bizarre Fig Cousin ▶━━

The strangler fig has a cousin that is just as odd as the strangler fig in its own way. It's the banyan tree of Asia, also a member of the fig family. It starts life in the same way as the strangler fig. A bird or other animal leaves a seed in the top of a tree, often a palm tree. When the seed sprouts, an aerial root grows down to the ground. But after this its growth is different from that of the strangler fig. The branches of the banyan tree grow outward, far beyond the host tree. Roots sprout from the underside of the branches and grow to the ground. In time each of these roots develops into a trunklike support for its branch. These supports can get as large as the trunk of a big oak tree. A single banyan tree may have 200 or 300 such props, so that it looks like a forest. It's said that 7,000 men in the army of Alexander the Great camped under one banyan tree in India.

banyan tree

Resources

Some of the plants in this book can be ordered from the following biological supply companies:

Carolina Biological Supply Company
2700 York Road
Burlington, NC 27215
Phone: 800 334-5551 (U.S.),
336 584-0381 (International)
http://www.carolina.com
E-mail: carolina@carolina.com

Ward's Natural Science Establishment
P.O. Box 92912
5100 West Henrietta Road
Rochester, NY 14692
Phone: 800 962-2660
http://www.wardsci.com
E-mail: customer_service@wardsci.com

You can order seeds from the following companies. They publish seed catalogs and provide seeds to botanical gardens as well as to the public.

Burpee Seed
300 Park Avenue
Warminster, PA 18974
Phone: 800 888-1447
http://www.burpee.com

Mellinger's
2310 West South Range Road
North Lima, OH 44452
Phone: 800 321-7444
http://www.mellingers.com
E-mail: mellgarden@aol.com

Park Seed
1 Parkton Avenue
Greenwood, SC 29647
Phone: 800 845-3369
http://www.parkseed.com

To find the name and location of a botanical garden or arboretum near you, contact the American Association of Botanical Gardens and Arboreta (AABGA). Or look at the list of gardens and their addresses at this Web site: http://www.ahta.org/otherht.html. There are hundreds of botanical gardens open to the public in the United States and Canada. The AABGA has a directory that you can order.

AABGA
351 Longwood Road
Kennett Square, PA 19348
Fax: 610 925-2700
Phone: 610 925-2500
http://www.aabga.org

To find a list of children's gardens, visit this Web site: http://gardennet.com. When you get to the home page, just click on Garden Guide Book. Then click on Browse Gardens by Type. Then click on Children's Gardens. You will find a list of over 30 children's gardens, with details about admission, garden features, and activities.

Here are the addresses of a few botanical gardens and arboreta in the United States and Canada.

The Arnold Arboretum at Harvard
  University
125 Arborway
Jamaica Plain, MA 02130-3519
Phone: 617 524-1718
http://arboretum.harvard.edu
E-mail: arbweb@arnarb.harvard.edu

Atlanta Botanical Garden
1345 Piedmont Avenue
Atlanta, GA 30309
Phone: 404 876-5859
http://www.atlantabotanicalgarden.org

Butchart Gardens
Box 4010
Victoria, BC
Canada V8X 3X4
Fax: 250 652-3883
Phone: 250 652-4422
http://www.butchartgardens.com

Callaway Gardens
P.O. Box 2000
Pine Mountain, GA 31822-2000
Phone: 800-CALLAWAY
http://www.callawaygardens.com

Chicago Botanic Garden
1000 Lake Cook Road
Glencoe, IL 60022
Phone: 847 835-8211, 835-8215
http://www.chicago-botanic.org

Denver Botanic Garden
909 York Street
Denver, CO 80206
Fax: 303 331-4013
Phone: 303 331-4000

Fairchild Tropical Garden
10901 Old Cutter Road
Coral Gables (Miami), FL 33156
Phone: 305 667-1651
http://www.ftg.org

Huntington Botanical Gardens
1151 Oxford Road
San Marino, CA 91108
Phone: 626 405-2100
http://www.huntington.org

Longwood Gardens
Route 1, P.O. Box 501
Kennett Square, PA 19348-0501
Phone: 616 388-1000
http://www.longwoodgardens.org

Missouri Botanical Garden
P.O. Box 299
4344 Shaw Boulevard
St. Louis, MO 63166-0299
Phone: 800 642-8842
http://www.mobot.org

Montréal Botanical Garden
4101 Sherbrooke East
Montréal, Québec
Canada
H1X 2B2
Phone: 514 872-1400
http://www.ville.montreal.qc.ca/jardin/
  en/menu.htm

Morton Arboretum
4100 Illinois Route 53
Lisle, IL 60532
Phone: 630 968-0074, 719-2400
http://www.mortonarb.org
E-mail: trees@mortonarb.org

New York Botanical Garden
200th Street and Kazimiroff Boulevard
Bronx, NY 10458-5126
Phone: 718 817-8649
http://www.nybg.org

San Antonio Botanical Gardens
555 Funston Place
San Antonio, TX 78209
Phone: 210 207-3263
http://www.sabot.org

Glossary

aerial root   A root that passes through air before penetrating the ground. (See also prop root.)

alternation of generations   The alternation of gametophyte and sporophyte generations in the life cycle of a plant.

anther   The upper part of a stamen, containing the pollen grains.

aquatic   Living in or on water.

asexual reproduction   Any reproduction that does not involve the union of sperm and egg.

blade   The broad, expanded part of a leaf. The term is also used to refer to the leaflike structures of kelp.

bog   An open and continually waterlogged area where the ground is covered with peat and sphagnum mosses.

botanist   A scientist who specializes in the study of plants.

bud   An immature flower that has not opened yet, or a stem or leaf that is just beginning to grow.

budding   A form of reproduction whereby a new plant develops on the side of a mature plant, then breaks free.

bulbil   A small, round plant part that can grow into a new plant (see fern chapter).

calyx   The outermost or lowest part of a flower, composed of leaflike sepals.

camouflage   A means of hiding whereby the coloring, texture, shape, or behavior of a living thing makes it appear to be part of its natural surroundings.

carbohydrate   Any of a group of compounds that include sugars and starches and are composed of carbon, hydrogen, and oxygen.

carnivore   A meat-eating or flesh-eating animal or plant.

carnivorous   Meat-eating. The meat eaten by carnivorous plants is often the bodies of insects.

carrion   Dead and rotting flesh.

carrion flies   Flies that lay their eggs on carrion. Their larvae feed on the carrion until they pupate.

cell   The smallest unit of a living thing that is capable of functioning independently. It consists of an outer cell membrane, which encloses a nucleus, cytoplasm, and several smaller structures called organelles.

chlorophyll   Green pigments located in the cells of leaves and stems. These pigments absorb energy from the Sun, which fuels the process of photosynthesis.

chloroplast   A structure inside some plant cells that contains chlorophylls necessary for photosynthesis to occur.

coevolution   Hereditary changes that develop over a long period of interaction between two species. A predator may change to hunt a prey species more efficiently. The prey species may change to become more effectively camouflaged. Or two species may change to take better advantage of a cooperative partnership between the two.

coevolve   For two species of organisms to change and develop new hereditary characteristics, over a long period of time, in response to the interaction between them.

cold-blooded   Having a body temperature that varies with the temperature of the surroundings; not warm-blooded. All animals other than birds and mammals are cold-blooded.

column   An organ found in the flowers of orchids that results from the evolutionary fusion of male stamens and female styles and stigmas.

community   A group of organisms living together and interacting with each other in a natural habitat.

cone   Scaly, rounded structures that produce pollen and seeds, characteristic of plants in the phylum Coniferophyta.

corm   A short, thickened underground stem, upright in position, in which food is stored for a plant.

corolla   The ring of petals on a flower.

corsage   A small bunch of flowers worn pinned to the front of a dress or a suit.

court   In animals, to communicate interest in mating to a potential partner.

crustacean   Any of various joint-legged animals of the class Crustacea, most of which are aquatic. This class includes lobsters, crabs, pill bugs, crayfish, and many very tiny animals.

deciduous   Describes broad-leaved trees or shrubs that drop their leaves at the end of each growing season.

dispersal   The spreading out of offspring to avoid crowding and competition.

dormant   In a period without activity or growth.

drip tip   The pointed tip of many rain forest leaves, which hangs toward the ground and encourages water from the surface of the leaf to drip off, slowing the growth of parasites and epiphytes on the leaf's surface.

ecosystem   A community of living things and their environment interacting and functioning as a unit.

egg   In plants, a single cell that is capable of being fertilized, and will then develop into an embryo and eventually into an adult plant.

embryo   An organism in the very early stages of development.

enzyme A protein that causes or facilitates a reaction between two other chemical substances. Enzymes are necessary to many of the reactions involved in the chemical processes of living.

epiphyte   A plant that grows on another plant, but is not parasitic on it. It does not steal food from the plant it grows on.

estuary   The wide area of a river where it runs into the ocean. Ocean tides run into an estuary, and the water is a mixture of freshwater and salt water.

euglossine bees   Bees belonging to the tribe Euglossini, which are known for pollinating orchids. They are also called orchid bees.

evaporate   To move from a liquid to a gaseous state. When water evaporates, it becomes the gas called water vapor.

evergreen   Describes plants that keep their leaves or needles all year round, rather than dropping them at the end of summer or autumn as deciduous plants do.

evolution   The process of hereditary changes in a species occurring in response to changes in the species' environment.

evolutionary time   The thousands or millions of years that are often necessary for significant genetic changes to occur within a population or species.

evolve   To change or develop gradually over thousands or millions of years. The term refers to genetic or hereditary changes in species of living things.

exoskeleton   The hard outer covering or skin of an animal in the phylum Arthropoda, which includes insects and crustaceans. An exoskeleton provides support and protection, and is shed periodically as growth occurs.

family   A category of biological classification ranking above a genus and below an order, and usually composed of several genera.

fertilization   The union of a sperm and an egg, resulting in the development of a new organism.

filament   The stalk of the stamen, which supports the anther.

flower   The reproductive structure of plants in the phylum Anthophyta, the flowering plants.

food web   A diagram showing the dietary relationships among all of the living things in a given community or ecosystem. It shows predator-prey and herbivore-plant relationships.

frond   The leaf of a fern. Sometimes the term is used to refer to the stipe and blades of kelp.

fruit   The ripened ovary of a flowering plant, containing the seeds.

fruit dot   A casual term for a sorus, a cluster of sporangia on the underside of a fern frond. The reproductive spores are released from the fruit dot, or sorus.

gamete   A sperm or an egg. In primitive living things, gametes can be any two cells that join together to produce a new organism.

gametophyte   In plants with alternation of generations, the gametophyte is the life stage that produces the gametes, or the sperm and egg.

gemma (plural **gemmae**)   Budlike structures in liverworts and mosses that detach and may develop into new plants.

genus (plural **genera**)   A category of biological classification ranking above a species and below a family, and composed of related species.

germinate   To begin growth, as in a seed or spore.

habitat   The natural environment that an animal lives in.

herbivore   An animal that eats plants.

herbivorous   Living on a diet of plants.

holdfast   The rootlike structures at the base of kelp that anchor it to the rocks on the ocean floor.

holoparasite   A living thing that is entirely parasitic, getting all of its nourishment from another living thing.

hormone   A chemical produced by the cells of a living thing that governs the functioning of its own body.

host   The living animal, plant, or fungus that a parasite feeds upon.

inflorescence   A cluster of flowers on a plant.

keystone species   A species whose presence is particularly important to the survival of other species in its community. When a keystone species is removed, the relationships among the other organisms in the community often collapse and extinctions occur.

labellum   One of the three petals of an orchid. It is located between the other two, and is usually larger and different in shape from them. It often serves as a landing platform for pollinating insects.

leaf (plural **leaves**)   A usually green and flat plant structure whose function is photosynthesis and the regulation of gas exchange and water balance.

lip   See labellum.

mammal   An animal with a backbone that is warm-blooded and, when female, produces milk for its young.

mutualism   A cooperative relationship between two species that benefits both species. As an adjective, **mutualistic**.

natural selection   The principle that individuals having characteristics that improve survival will live longer and produce more offspring, and that the proportion of individuals having these characteristics will increase with each successive generation.

nectar   A sugary liquid produced by flowers which attracts pollinators.

needle   The thin, often stiff, needle-shaped leaf produced by many cone-bearing trees.

nutrients   Substances in the foods of living things that are necessary for health.

ovary   The swollen, roundish, basal part of a pistil, containing the ovules or seeds.

ovule   A structure containing an egg or an embryo and the tissues necessary for the beginning growth of the embryo. After fertilization, the ovule develops into a seed.

parasite   In plants, a parasite is a plant that lives and feeds on another living plant, robbing it of nutrients.

parasitize   In plants, to live on another living plant, stealing nutrients from inside the other plant.

peat   The accumulation of partly decomposed vegetation, especially sphagnum mosses.

petal   A leaflike segment of the corolla of a flower, often brightly colored to attract pollinators.

petiole   The stem that attaches the blade of a leaf to the rest of the plant.

pheromone   A chemical produced by a living thing that influences the behavior of other individuals of the same species.

photosynthesis   The production of sugar from carbon dioxide and water in the presence of the pigment chlorophyll, using light energy and releasing oxygen.

phylum (plural **phyla**)   A category of biological classification, ranking below a kingdom and above a class.

pistil   The female organ in the center of a flower, consisting of a stigma, a style, and an ovary that contains ovules.

plankton   Microscopic living things that float or drift in great numbers in bodies of water.

plant   A living thing that typically produces its own food by photosynthesis and has many specialized cells with different functions. The cells of plants are covered with cell walls instead of the cell membranes that cover the cells of animals.

pollen   Tiny, dustlike, usually yellow grains produced by the male part of a flower. Each grain contains two living sperm cells.

pollinate   To transfer pollen from the anther to the stigma of the same or another flower.

pollination   The transfer of pollen from the anther of one flower to the stigma of another flower (or occasionally the same flower).

pollinator   An animal that transfers pollen from the anther of one flower to the stigma of another flower (or occasionally the same flower).

pollinium (plural **pollinia**)   A compact mass of pollen produced by some flowers, such as orchids.

predator   An animal that catches living animals and eats them.

prey   A living animal caught and eaten by another animal.

prothallus (plural **prothalli**)   In ferns and some other lower plants, the free-living or independent gametophyte generation, which produces sperm and eggs.

prop root (aerial root)   A root that passes through air and maybe water before entering the ground. It may provide support for the plant, and may have openings for gas exchange. Most plants lack prop roots, but they are abundant in mangrove trees, banyan trees, and some others.

pupa   The stage of insect development following the larval stage, where transformation to the adult stage occurs.

rhizoid   Slender, hairlike structures similar to root hairs. Their function is attachment and absorption of water or nutrients in many kinds of plants.

rhizome   An underground stem that is usually horizontal and is the main stem of the plant. Often it is thickened and contains stored food. Rhizomes may have buds and scalelike leaves.

root   The part of a plant, usually underground, that supports and anchors the plant and draws water and nutrients from the soil.

root hairs   Tiny hairlike outgrowths of roots.

rootlet   A small root.

rosette   An arrangement of leaves radiating from a central point, usually on the ground.

scavenger   An animal that feeds on already dead plant or animal matter.

secrete   To produce and get rid of bodily fluids.

sepal   A leaflike structure that is part of the calyx, the outermost part of a flower bud and the lowest ring of structures on a mature flower.

semiparasite   In plants, a plant that gets some of its nutrition by stealing from other plants, but produces some of its food by photosynthesis.

sorus (plural **sori**)   A cluster of sporangia on the underside of a fern frond. The reproductive spores are released from the sori.

spadix   A fleshy spike in which flowers are imbedded, as in the arum family.

spathe   A modified leaf that surrounds a cluster of flowers.

sperm   A male reproductive cell capable of fertilizing an egg.

sporangium (plural **sporangia**)   A spore case in which spores are formed. They are clustered in the sori on the undersides of some fern fronds.

spore   A very, very tiny reproductive body produced by some lower plants. Unlike a seed, a spore does not contain any protection or nutrition. It usually consists of only one cell.

sporophyte   In some plants, the part of the life cycle that produces sporangia and spores.

stamen   The male reproductive part of a flower, consisting of a filament and an anther containing pollen.

stem   The main stalk of some plants. The term also refers to a plant part supporting another plant part, such as a flower.

stigma   The sticky top surface of the pistil of a flower.

stipe   The stemlike part of an alga such as kelp.

stoma (plural **stomata**)   An opening or pore in a leaf or stem, between two specialized cells called guard cells, which can open or close the opening. Water vapor, carbon dioxide, and oxygen pass through the stomata.

style   The long, slender part of a pistil that connects the ovary and the stigma.

subtropical   Having a very warm climate, but not as warm as tropical areas. Subtropical areas lie in between the tropics (which are on or near the equator) and temperate climates.

subtropics   Areas of the earth that have a subtropical climate.

symbiosis   The close association of two unrelated organisms. The relationship is helpful to one partner, and may be helpful, harmful, or neither to the other.

temperate   Having a mild or moderate climate. Temperate zones are often found midway between the equator and the poles.

terrestrial   Living on land.

thallus (plural **thalli**)   A type of plant body that does not have distinct leaves, stems, or roots.

tropical   Having a hot and humid climate; being on or relatively near the equator.

tropics   Areas of the earth that have a tropical climate.

tundra   A treeless area of Arctic regions. The ground is permanently frozen except for the top few inches, which thaw in summer. It is covered with low-lying plants.

turion   A reproductive body produced by duckweed plants, which overwinters in a dormant state underwater.

variety   A category of classification in plants, ranking below a species. One species of an ornamental or a cultivated plant may have several varieties. This applies particularly to popular plants such as orchids, roses, and apples.

vascular system   A system of vessels in vascular plants that is vaguely similar to our circulatory system, but without a pump. The vessels conduct water, dissolved minerals, and sugars to cells throughout the plant.

vegetative reproduction   Asexual reproduction, or reproduction that does not involve male and female parts.

warm-blooded   Applies to birds and mammals, which have a constant body temperature that is generated and regulated internally and is independent of the temperature of the environment.

whorl   Three or more leaves or branches growing from a central spot. The term can apply to the parts of a flower, as a whorl of petals or a whorl of sepals or a whorl of stamens.

Index _____

acacia trees, 92-95
aerial root, 66, 110-11, 112, 115
Africa, 15, 95, 100
agouti, 112
air pineapples, 30
Alabama, 69
Alaska, 87, 99, 100, 108
Aleutian Islands, 99
Alexander the Great, 112
algae, 3, 6, 27, 68, 96-100
alternation of generations, 13, 14, 115
animals
  as carriers, 4, 27, 37
  duckweed, 25, 26, 27
  epiphytes, 29, 30, 31
  giant kelp forests, 96, 97, 98–100
  giant sequoias, 60
  herbivores, 2
  mangrove swamps, 65, 66, 68–70
  mutualism, 95
  pitcher plants, 54, 57
  saguaro cactus, 79, 80
  strangler figs, 110, 111, 112
Antarctic, 15, 22, 41, 91
anther, 3, 35, 115
ant plant, 31
ants, 31, 92, 93–95, 112
aquatic plants, 115
  bladderwort, 89–91
  duckweed, 24–28
  ferns, 19
  as first on earth, 21
  giant Amazon water lilies, 85–88
  giant kelp forests, 96–100
  mangroves, 65–70
Araceae (arum) family, 6, 10, 11, 12
arboreta, 113, 114
Arctic, 15, 41, 75, 91
Argentina, 16, 86, 87
Arizona, 77, 78, 80, 81, 82
arum (Araceae) family, 6, 10, 11, 12
asexual reproduction, 15, 21, 51, 115
Asia, 15, 52, 99, 102, 112
aster family (Asteraceae), 6, 38
Atlantic Ocean, 55
Atlantic ridley sea turtle, 70
Australia, 15, 100, 105, 108
Azolla fern, 19

Baja California, 100
bald eagle, 69
banyan tree, 112
bats, 80, 82, 110, 112
bees, 10, 73, 74–75, 111–12
Belt, Thomas, 94
Beltian bodies, 94
Bering Sea, 99, 100
birds
  duckweed, 25, 26, 27
  epiphyte, 30, 31
  mangroves, 68, 69, 70
  mistletoe, 39, 40, 41
  mutualism, 95
  saguaro cactus, 79, 80, 81, 82
  strangler figs, 110, 111, 112
  titan arum, 103
black-eyed Susan, 38
bladderworts, 89–91
bladder wrack (rockweed), 96
blade, 97, 98, 115
bog, 16, 55, 115
Bolivia, 86
botanical gardens, 87, 113, 114
botanist, 90, 115
Brazil, 86
bristlecone pine trees, 64
bromeliads, 29–30, 31, 32, 33
brown algae, 96–97
brown pelicans, 69
bucket orchids, 74–75
bud, 78, 86, 101, 104, 115
budding, 25, 115
bulbil, 21, 115
bull's-horn acacia, 93
bumblebee orchid, 73

cactus, 5, 77–82
Caladenia orchid, 73
Calaveras Big Trees State Park, 63
calcium oxalate, 11
California
  bristlecone pine trees, 64
  cobra plant, 55, 56
  giant sequoias, 62–63
  kelp forest, 100
  orchids, 76
  redwood trees, 62
  sea otters, 100
  water lilies, 87
calyx, 5, 115
camouflage, 41, 115
carbohydrate, 30, 115

carbon dioxide, 30, 40
Carboniferous period, 3, 19
carnivore, 46, 115
carnivorous plants, 52, 75, 115
  bladderwort, 89–91
  pitcher plant, 31, 53–58
  sundew plant, 48–52
  Venus's-flytrap, 45–47
carpenter ants, 112
carrion, 101, 115
carrion flies, 102, 115
cell, 115
Central America, 15, 22, 95
Cephalotus, 56
chickaree, 60
children's gardens, 113
Chiloglottis orchid, 73
chlorophyll, 96, 106, 108, 115
chloroplast, 5, 115
Christmas star orchid, 76
Christmas tree, 42
chrysanthemum, 38
classification, plant, 6
club mosses, 3, 22
coast redwoods, 61, 62
cobra plant, 55, 56
cocklebur, 37
coconut, 37
coconut palm tree, 80
coevolution, 95, 115
coevolve, 115
cold-blooded, 11, 115
color in plants, 5, 38
Colorado, 87
column, 73, 115
community, 98, 115
cone, 3, 4, 115
  bristlecone pine, 64
  giant sequoia, 59–60
  redwood, 62
corm, 12, 103, 115
corolla, 5, 115
corsage, 72, 116
Coryanthes speciosa orchid, 74–75
court, 116
cow lily, 87
crabs, 31, 65, 68, 98
crocodiles, 70
crustacean, 26, 68, 98, 116
Cryptanthemis slateri orchid, 108
Crystal Palace (London), 85
cycads, 18, 19
Cyclocephala beetles, 88

daisy, 6, 38
dandelions, 34–38
Darwin, Charles, 23, 49, 52, 76
deciduous, 108, 116
Dendrobates, 29
desert cactus, 77, 78
dinosaurs, 3, 18
disk flowers, 38
dispersal, 5, 68, 116
dormant, 25, 116
Drakaea orchid, 71, 73
drip tip, 15, 32, 116
ducks, 25, 26
duckweeds, 24–28
dwarf mistletoe, 40, 41

eagles, 69
ecosystem, 70, 116
egg, 3, 4, 116
egrets, reddish, 69
elf owl, 80
embryo, 4, 5, 116
Emmons, Louise, 102
endangerment
  cactuses, 82
  carnivorous plants, 47, 57
  mangrove swamps, 70
  orchids, 71
  peat bogs, 16
  sea otters, 99–100
  sequoias redwoods, 63
  wetlands, 58
England, 16, 85, 86
enzyme, 50, 55, 116
epiphyte, 29–33, 116
  bladderworts, 91
  ferns, 19
  mosses, 15
  orchids, 72, 76
Estes, James, 99
estuary, 69, 116
eucalyptus trees, 107
euglossine (orchid) bees, 74–75, 116
Europe, 16
evaporate, 11, 116
evergreen, 59, 116
evolution, 52, 116
  coevolution, 95
evolutionary time, 116
evolve, 116
exoskeleton, 46, 116

falcon, peregrine, 69
family, 6, 116
ferns, 3, 18–23

alternation of generations, 13
  as epiphytes, 29
  habitat, 32
fertilization, 36, 74, 116
filament, 3, 116
fish
  bladderwort, 89, 91
  duckweed, 26
  giant kelp forests, 98
  mangroves, 68, 70
  mutualism, 95
  overfishing, 70, 99, 100
flicker, gilded, 79, 80
flies, 10, 101–2, 103, 107
Florida
  mangroves, 65–70
  orchids, 76
  Spanish moss, 32, 33
  strangler figs, 112
Florida panthers, 66, 70
flower, 3–5, 116
  bladderwort, 90
  Christmas tree, 42
  dandelion, 34, 35
  duckweed, 24, 25
  giant Amazon water lily, 86, 88
  Indian pipe, 108
  jack-in-the-pulpit, 12
  mangroves, 67
  orchids, 72–73
  parts of, 3–5
  pitcher plants, 54, 55
  rafflesias, 101–2, 104
  saguaro cactus, 78
  skunk cabbage, 9
  sundew plant, 49
  underground orchids, 105, 107
  water lilies, 87
  world's largest, 103
food web, 2, 116
  of mangroves, 68, 70
forest fires, 61
frogs, 29, 31
frond, 19, 32, 97, 116
fruit, 116
  duckweed, 25
  flower-bearing plants, 4–5
  giant Amazon water lilies, 88
  jack-in-the-pulpit, 12
  mangroves, 67
  mistletoe, 39, 40, 42
  rafflesia, 102

saguaro cactus, 78, 80
strangler figs, 110
titan arum, 103
world's smallest, 24
fruit dot (sori), 20, 116
fuel, 2, 16
fungus, 95, 105, 107, 108, 111

gamete, 14, 116
gametophyte, 117
  ferns, 20–21
  mosses, 14, 15
Gardner, C. A., 105
gases, 2, 30, 32
gemma, 15, 117
General Grant tree, 63
General Sherman tree, 63
genus, 6, 117
germinate, 4, 117
giant Amazon water lilies, 85–88
giant kelp, 6, 80, 96–100
giant sequoias, 59–64
gila woodpecker, 79–80
gilded flickers, 79, 80
gland
  mangroves, 67
  pitcher plants, 55
  sundews, 48, 49–50
  Venus's-flytrap, 46
greater duckweed, 24
great horned owl, 79
great white herons, 69
great yellow pond lily, 87
green algae, 96
guard hairs, 46, 91
Guiana, 86
Gulf of Mexico, 55, 66

habitat, 68, 117
Haenke, Thaddäus, 86
Harris' hawk, 79, 81
haustoria, 104
heat, 10–11, 88
Heliamphora, 56
herbivore, 2, 117
herbivorous, 117
herons, great white, 69
hog-waste lagoons, 27
Hoh Rainforest, 32
holdfast, 97, 98, 117
holoparasite, 40, 117
hood
  cobra plants, 56
  jack-in-the-pulpit, 12, 25
  pitcher plants, 53, 55, 58
  skunk cabbage, 9, 10, 11, 25
  titan arum, 25

hormone, 41, 117
hornbills, 103
horsetail, 3, 19, 22
host, 40, 41, 117
hummingbirds, 4, 30
hydra, 26
hydrozoa, 14

India, 112
Indian Ocean, 56
Indian pipe, 108
Indonesia, 56, 102, 103
inflorescence, 117
  world's largest, 103
Insectivorous Plants (Darwin),
  52
insects, 4
  acacia tree, 92, 93–95
  bladderwort, 91
  duckweed, 26
  epiphytes, 30, 31
  giant Amazon water lilies,
    88
  giant sequoia trees, 60, 61
  mistletoe leaves, 41
  orchids, 71, 73–75, 76
  pitcher plants, 53, 54, 55,
    57
  as pollinators, 5, 38
  rafflesias, 101–2
  redwood trees, 61
  saguaro cactus, 80
  skunk cabbage, 10–11
  strangler figs, 111–12
  sundew plant, 48–50
  titan arum, 103
  underground orchids, 107
  Venus's-flytrap, 46
Inyo National Forest, 64
Ireland, 16

jack-in-the-pulpit, 6, 11, 12
Janzen, Daniel, 94–95
jellyfish, 13, 14
juniper trees, 41
Jurassic, 18

kelp, 80, 96–100
keystone species, 80–81, 117
killer whales, 99, 100
kingdoms, 6
Kings Canyon National Park,
  63

labellum, 73, 117
lady's slipper, 71, 74, 75, 76
lake ferns, 19

leaf, 117
  acacia, 93
  bromeliad, 30
  dandelion, 35, 36
  duckweed, 24, 25
  fern, 19
  giant Amazon water lily,
    85–86
  mistletoe, 39
  mosses, 13
  photosynthesis, 2, 5
  pitcher plants, 53, 54
  role of, 5
  skunk cabbage, 9–10
  Spanish moss, 33
  strangler fig, 111
  sundew plant, 48
  titan arum, 103
  Venus's-flytrap, 45, 46
  water lily, 87
leafy mistletoe, 40
legume family, 93
Lemnaceae, 24
lenticel, 67, 69
lesser duckweed, 24
lettuce, 38
lichen, 15, 32
Liliaceae family, 87
lily pads, 87
lip. *See* labellum
liverwort, 15
lizards, 31, 68, 69, 80, 112
logging, 61, 62, 63
Longwood Gardens, 87
Louisiana, 69

Macrocystis pyrifera, 97
Madagascar, 54, 56, 76
Malaysia
  orchids, 76
  pitcher plants, 54, 56
  rafflesias, 102
  tree ferns, 22
mammal 27, 31, 37 60, 66,
    68, 80, 94, 95, 96, 98–100,
    109, 110, 112, 117
mangroves, 65–70
  ant plants, 31
  as keystone species, 80
  seeds of, 37
mangrove swamps, 68, 80
marigold, 38
McIvor, Carole C., 69
medusa, 14
Mexico, 81, 108
mice, 80
milkweed, 37

mineral nutrients, 5, 6, 33
Mississippi, 69
Missouri, 87
Missouri Botanical Garden,
  87
mistletoe, 39–42, 72
monkeys, 54, 110, 111, 112
Monterey Bay Aquarium, 100
mosses, 3, 13–17, 22, 32, 91
moths, orchids, 76
Muir Woods National
  Monument, 62
mutualism, 95, 117

Nais, Jamili, 102
National Marine Fisheries
  Service, 100
national parks, 32, 62, 63, 82
natural selection, 52, 117
nectar, 4, 117
  acacia trees, 94
  Christmas star orchid, 80
  pitcher plants, 55
  saguaro cactus, 80, 82
  Venus's-flytrap, 46
needles, 62, 64, 117
Nepenthes, 54, 56
New York, 87
New York Botanical Garden,
  87
New Zealand, 22
nitrogen, 49, 55
North Carolina, 11, 46
Nuphar water lily, 87
nutrients, 31, 104, 111, 117
Nymphaeaceae family, 87

odor, 4
  giant Amazon water lily, 88
  orchid, 71
  pitcher plant, 55
  rafflesia, 101–2
  skunk cabbage, 10, 11
  sundew, 49
  titan arum, 103
Odum, William E., 69
oil spills, 99
Olympic National Park, 32
Ophrys orchid, 73
Orchidaceae family, 72
orchids, 29, 71–76
  habitat, 32
  underground, 105–8
Oregon, 55, 100
osprey, 69, 79
ovary, 4, 5, 37, 38, 117
ovule, 4, 117

owls, 79, 80
oxygen, 2, 67

Pacific Ocean, 80
palm trees, 32, 109
parasite, 117
　Christmas tree as, 42
　Indian pipe as, 108
　mistletoe as, 40, 41, 42
　rafflesia as, 104
　underground orchids as,
　　106–7
parasitize, 41, 104, 117
parrot pitcher, 54
Paxton, Joseph, 85, 86–87
peat, 51, 16, 117
peccaries, 112
pelicans, brown, 69
Pennsylvania, 87
peregrine falcon, 69
petal, 4, 5, 73, 117
petiole, 51, 117
pheromone, 71, 117
Philippines, 102
Phoradendron flavescens, 39
photosynthesis, 2, 4, 5, 30,
　　108, 117
　algae, 6
　cactus, 77–78
　mistletoe, 40
　orchids, 72, 106
phylum, 6, 118
Phymatodes nitidus beetle, 60
pine trees, 3, 46
　mistletoe parasite, 40, 41
　oldest living, 64
Pisaster starfish, 80–81
pistil, 4, 5, 35, 72–73, 88, 102,
　　118
pitcher plants, 31, 53–58
planarians, 26
plankton, 68, 118
plants, 2–6, 118
　ancient forests, 18–19
　classification, 6
　ordering, 113
　parts of, 3–6
　resources, 113–14
　role of, 2
poisonous, 42
pollen, 3, 4, 118
　giant Amazon water lily, 88
　orchid, 72, 73, 74, 75
　Rafflesia, 102
　underground orchids, 107
pollination, 10, 30, 71, 73–75,
　　118

pollinator, 5, 30, 118
pollinium, 73–74, 75, 118
pollution, 27, 99
ponds, 19, 27, 91
praedicta moth, 76
predator, 80, 118
prey, 2, 118
prop root, 118. *See also* aerial
　root
prothallus (gametophyte),
　　20–21, 23, 118
Protista kingdom, 96
purple pitcher, 54, 55

Raffles, Sir Thomas Stamford,
　　102
Rafflesia arnoldii, 101, 102
rafflesias, 72, 101–4
rain forests
　epiphytes, 30, 31–32
　mosses, 15
　orchids, 72
　rafflesias, 102
　strangler figs, 110
　titan arum, 103
ray flowers, 38
red algae, 96
reddish egrets, 69
Redwood National Park, 62
redwoods, 61, 62
reproduction, 3–4, 5
　asexual, 15, 21, 51, 115, 119
　by budding, 25
　dandelion, 36
　duckweed, 25
　experiments with, 23, 51,
　　57–58
　fern, 20–21
　giant Amazon water lily, 88
　giant sequoia, 62
　jack-in-the-pulpit, 12
　mangrove, 67–68
　moss, 14
　orchid, 72
　rafflesia, 102
　redwood, 62
　by seeds, 19–20
　skunk cabbage, 10
　by spores, 20
　sundew, 51
　underground orchid, 107
Rhizanthella gardneri orchid,
　　72, 105, 106, 107
Rhizoctonia fungus, 107
rhizoid, 13, 118
rhizome, 19, 21, 22, 23, 58,
　　106, 118

rivers, 27, 85
rockweed (bladder wrack), 96
root, 118
　banyan tree, 112
　dandelion, 36
　fern, 19
　jack-in-the-pulpit, 12
　mangrove, 66, 69
　pitcher plant, 57–58
　role of, 6
　sequoia redwood, 61
　strangler fig, 109, 110–11
root hairs, 6, 118
rootlet, 24–25, 118
roseate spoonbill, 68, 69
rosette, 45, 118
Russia, 16

saguaro cactus, 5, 77–82
Saguaro National Park, 82
salamanders, 31
salt water mangroves, 67
Sarracenia, 53, 54, 55
scarab beetles, 88
scavenger, 98, 118
Schulman, George, 64
scorpions, 80
Scotland
screech owls, 80
sea lions, 99, 100
seals, 99
sea otters, 97, 98–100
sea urchin barrens, 99
sea urchins, 98–100
seaweed, 96, 100
secrete, 118
seeds, 3, 4, 19–20
　acacia tree, 93
　dispersal in dandelions, 37
　dispersal in epiphytes, 31
　giant Amazon water lily, 86,
　　87, 88
　mangrove, 67–68
　mistletoe, 39, 40, 42
　ordering, 113
　rafflesia, 102
　saguaro cactus, 73
　strangler fig, 110
semiparasite, 118
　leafy mistletoe as, 40
sepal, 5, 118
Sequoia National Park, 63
shrimp, 68, 70
skunk cabbage, 6, 9–11
slugs, 11, 31, 98
smell. *See* odor
Smith, Thomas J., 69

snails, 26, 65, 68, 98
snakes, 31, 80
Sonoran Desert, 77, 78, 80, 81
sorus (fruit dot), 20, 118
South America, 81, 86, 87, 95,
    100, 112
South Carolina, 46
spadix, 118
    arum family, 10
    jack-in-the-pulpit, 12
    skunk cabbage, 9
    titan arum, 103
Spanish moss, 32, 33
spathe, 11, 25, 103, 118
species, 6
sperm, 3, 4, 14, 118
sphagnum bogs, 16,
sphagnum moss, 16, 51, 57
spines, cactus, 77
sporangium, 20, 118
spore, 14, 15, 20, 118
sporophyte, 13, 14, 119
Sri Lanka, 54, 56
stalk
    flowering plants, 3
    giant kelp, 97
    sundew plant, 48
    underground orchid, 106
stamen, 3, 5, 119
starches, 2
starfish, 80–81
stem, 119
    bladderwort, 90
    fern, 19, 21
    horsetail, 22
    photosynthesis, 2
    role of, 5
    underground orchid, 106
sticktight, 37
stigma, 4, 35, 37, 88, 119
stipe, 97, 119
stoma, 5, 32, 119
strangler figs, 109–12
streams, 11, 15, 17
style, 4, 119
subtropical, 72, 119
subtropics, 119
    epiphytes, 32, 33
    orchids, 72, 75–76
    strangler figs, 112
    whisk ferns, 22
sugar, 2, 5, 30, 40, 77
Sumatra, 102, 103
sundew plants, 48–52
sunflower, 38
sunlight, 2, 30, 40, 46, 72, 77,
    78

swamps
    mangrove, 68, 69
    pitcher plants, 55
    skunk cabbages, 11
symbiosis, 119

tank bromeliad, 29–30, 31
tannin, 61
taproot, 36
Taxodiaceae family, 62
temperate, 30, 119
temperate rain forests, 30, 32
termites, 107
terrestrial, 90, 119
Tetrastigma vine, 104
Texas, 69
Thailand, 27, 102
thallus, 24, 119
thistle, 37, 38
thorns, acacia trees, 93
titan arum, 6, 25, 103
traps
    bladderwort, 89–91
    orchid, 74, 75
    Venus's-flytrap, 46
tree ferns, 19, 22
trees
    acacia, 92–95
    age rings, 60–61
    ancient, 18
    banyan, 112
    bean family, 93
    Christmas tree, 42
    epiphytes growing on, 29,
        30–31, 32, 33
    ferns as, 19, 22
    giant sequoias, 59–64
    mangroves, 31, 37, 65–70,
        80
    mistletoe growing on, 39,
        40, 41, 42
    moss on, 13, 15
    oldest living, 63, 64
    palm, 32, 80
    pine, 3, 40, 41, 46, 64
    redwoods, 61, 62
    reproduction, 3
    strangler figs, 109–12
trigger hairs, 46, 91
tropical, 119
tropics, 72, 119
    acacia trees, 95
    epiphytes, 29, 32
    ferns, 22
    giant Amazon water lilies,
        85, 86–87
    mangroves, 69

mosses, 15, 22
orchids, 72, 75–76
rafflesias, 102
strangler figs, 112
vascular plants, 22
Trott, John, 105
trumpet pitchers, 53–54
tundra, 15, 119
turion, 25, 119
turtles, 26, 70

underground orchids, 105–8
Utricularia, 90

variety, 72, 119
vascular system, 5, 21, 22,
    119
vegetative reproduction, 15,
    21, 51, 115
Venus's-flytrap, 45–47
vessels, in ferns, 21
*Victoria amazonica/Victoria
    cruziana,* 87
vines, 104
Virginia, 33
Viscum album, 39

warm-blooded, 98, 119
Washington State, 30, 32, 80,
    100
wasps, 71, 73–74, 111
water, 3
    absorption of, 13, 21, 31–32
    cactus storage of, 78–79
    movement within plants, 5,
        6
    See also aquatic plants
water lilies, 85–88
watermeal, 24
Web sites, 82, 113, 114
weed, dandelion as, 34–38
wetlands, 55, 58
whisk fern, 22
whorl, 22, 119
wind, 3, 4, 5, 31, 37
Wolffia, 24, 27
woodlands, 15, 108
woodpeckers, 79–80
worms, 28, 31, 98

Yosemite National Park, 63

zinnia, 38